BOOK 2

English
No Problem!®

Maria H. Koonce
Adult ESOL
Broward County Schools, FL

William J. Koonce
Adult ESOL
Nova Community School, FL

New Readers Press

English—No Problem®
English—No Problem! Level 2 Student Book
ISBN 978-1-56420-357-1

Copyright © 2004 New Readers Press
New Readers Press
ProLiteracy's Publishing Division
101 Wyoming Street, Syracuse, New York 13204
www.newreaderspress.com

Printed in the United States of America
19   18   17   16   15   14   13   12   11   10

Proceeds from the sale of New Readers Press materials support professional development, training, and technical assistance programs of ProLiteracy that benefit local literacy programs in the U.S. and around the globe.

Acquisitions Editor: Paula L. Schlusberg
Developer: Mendoza and Associates
Project Director: Roseanne Mendoza
Project Editor: Pat Harrington-Wydell
Content Editor: Terrie Lipke
Production Director: Heather Witt-Badoud
Designer: Kimbrly Koennecke
Illustrations: Carolyn Boehmer, Matt Terry, Linda Tiff, James Wallace
Production Specialist: Alexander R. Jones
Cover Design: Kimbrly Koennecke
Cover Photography: Robert Mescavage Photography
Photo Credits: Robert Mescavage Photography

Authors

Maria H. Koonce
Adult ESOL
Broward County Schools, FL

William J. Koonce
Adult ESOL
Nova Community School, FL

Contributors

National Council Members
Audrey Abed, *San Marcos Even Start Program, San Marcos, TX*
Myra K. Baum, *New York City Board of Education (retired), New York, NY*
Kathryn Hamilton, *Elk Grove Adult and Community Education, Sacramento, CA*
Brigitte Marshall, *Oakland Adult Education Programs, Oakland, CA*
Teri McLean, *Florida Human Resources Development Center, Gainesville, FL*
Alan Seaman, *Wheaton College, Wheaton, IL*

Reviewers
Sabrina Budasi-Martin, *William Rainey Harper College, Palatine, IL*
Linda Davis-Pluta, *Oakton Community College, Des Plaines, IL*
Patricia DeHesus-Lopez, *Center for Continuing Education, Texas A&M University, Kingsville, TX*
Gail Feinstein Forman, *San Diego City College, San Diego, CA*
Carolyn Harding, *Marshall High School Adult Program, Falls Church, VA*
Trish Kerns, *Old Marshall Adult Education Center, Sacramento City Unified School District, Sacramento, CA*
Debe Pack-Garcia, *Manteca Adult School, Humbolt, CA*
Pamela Patterson, *Seminole Community College, Sanford, FL*
Catherine Porter, *Adult Learning Resource Center, Des Plaines, IL*
Jean Rose, *ABC Adult School, Cerritos, CA*
Eric Rosenbaum, *Bronx Community College Adult Program, Bronx, NY*
Laurie Shapero, *Miami-Dade Community College, Miami, FL*
Terry Shearer, *North Harris College Community Education, Houston, TX*
Abigail Tom, *Durham Technical Community College, Chapel Hill, NC*

Pilot Teachers
Connie Bateman, *Gerber Adult Education Center, Sacramento, CA*
Jennifer Bell, *William Rainey Harper College, Palatine, IL*
Marguerite Bock, *Chula Vista Adult School, Chula Vista, CA*
Giza Braun, *National City Adult School, National City, CA*
Sabrina Budasi-Martin, *William Rainey Harper College, Palatine, IL*
Wong-Ling Chew, *Citizens Advice Bureau, Bronx, NY*
Renee Collins, *Elk Grove Adult and Community Education, Sacramento, CA*
Rosette Dawson, *North Harris College Community Education, Houston, TX*
Kathleen Edel, *Elk Grove Adult and Community Education, Sacramento, CA*
Margaret Erwin, *Elk Grove Adult and Community Education, Sacramento, CA*
Teresa L. Gonzalez, *North Harris College Community Education, Houston, TX*
Fernando L. Herbert, *Bronx Adult School, Bronx, NY*
Carolyn Killean, *North Harris College Community Education, Houston, TX*
Elizabeth Minicz, *William Rainey Harper College, Palatine, IL*

Larry Moore, *Long Beach Adult School, Long Beach, CA*
Lydia Omori, *William Rainey Harper College, Palatine, IL*
Valsa Panikulam, *William Rainey Harper College, Palatine, IL*
Kathryn Powell, *William Rainey Harper College, Palatine, IL*
Alan Reiff, *NYC Board of Education, Adult and Continuing Education, Bronx, NY*
Brenda M. Rodriguez, *San Marcos Even Start, San Marcos, TX*
Juan Carlos Rodriguez, *San Marcos Even Start, San Marcos, TX*
Joan Siff, *NYC Board of Education, Adult and Continuing Education, Bronx, NY*
Susie Simon, *Long Beach Adult School, Long Beach, CA*
Gina Tauber, *North Harris College, Houston, TX*
Diane Villanueva, *Elk Grove Adult and Community Education, Sacramento, CA*
Dona Wayment, *Elk Grove Adult and Community Education, Sacramento, CA*
Weihua Wen, *NYC Board of Education, Adult and Continuing Education, Bronx, NY*
Darla Wickard, *North Harris College Community Education, Houston, TX*
Judy Wurtz, *Sweetwater Union High School District, Chula Vista, CA*

Focus Group Participants
Leslie Jo Adams, *Laguna Niguel, CA*
Fiona Armstrong, *New York City Board of Education, New York, NY*
Myra K. Baum, *New York City Board of Education (retired), New York, NY*
Gretchen Bitterlin, *San Diego Unified School District, San Diego, CA*
Patricia DeHesus-Lopez, *Center for Continuing Education, Texas A&M University, Kingsville, TX*
Diana Della Costa, *Worksite ESOL Programs, Kissimmee, FL*
Frankie Dovel, *Orange County Public Schools, VESOL Program, Orlando, FL*
Marianne Dryden, *Region 1 Education Service Center, Edinburgh, TX*
Richard Firsten, *Lindsay Hopkins Technical Center, Miami, FL*
Pamela S. Forbes, *Bartlett High School, Elgin, IL*
Kathryn Hamilton, *Elk Grove Adult and Community Education, Sacramento, CA*
Trish Kerns, *Old Marshall Adult Education Center, Sacramento City Unified School District, Sacramento, CA*
Suzanne Leibman, *The College of Lake County, Grayslake, IL*
Patty Long, *Old Marshall Adult Education Center, Sacramento City Unified School District, Sacramento, CA*
Brigitte Marshall, *Oakland Adult Education Programs, Oakland, CA*
Bet Messmer, *Santa Clara Adult School, Santa Clara, CA*
Patricia Mooney, *New York State Board of Education, Albany, NY*
Lee Ann Moore, *Salinas Adult School, Salinas, CA*
Lynne Nicodemus, *San Juan Adult School, Carmichael, CA*
Pamela Patterson, *Seminole Community College, Sanford, FL*
Eric Rosenbaum, *Bronx Community College, Bronx, NY*
Linda Sasser, *Alhambra District Office, Alhambra, CA*
Federico Salas, *North Harris College Community Education, Houston, TX*
Alan Seaman, *Wheaton College, Wheaton, IL*
Kathleen Slattery, *Salinas Adult School, Salinas, CA*
Carol Speigl, *Center for Continuing Education, Texas A&M University, Kingsville, TX*
Edie Uber, *Santa Clara Adult School, Santa Clara, CA*
Lise Wanage, *CASAS, Phoenix, AZ*

Special thanks to Audrey Abed, Brigitte Marshall, and Teri McLean for their help in the development of this book.

About This Series

Meeting Adult Learners' Needs with *English—No Problem!*

English—No Problem! is a theme-based, performance-based series focused on developing critical thinking and cultural awareness and on building language and life skills. Designed for adult and young adult English language learners, the series addresses themes and issues meaningful to adults in the United States.

English—No Problem! is appropriate for and respectful of adult learners. These are some key features:
- interactive, communicative, participatory approach
- rich, authentic language
- problem-posing methodology
- project-based units and task-based lessons
- goal setting embedded in each unit and lesson
- units organized around themes of adult relevance
- contextualized, inductive grammar
- student materials designed to fit into lesson plans
- performance assessment, including tools for learner self-evaluation

Series Themes

Across the series, units have the following themes:
- Life Stages: Personal Growth and Goal Setting
- Making Connections
- Taking Care of Yourself
- Personal Finance
- Consumer Awareness
- Protecting Your Legal Rights
- Participating in Your New Country and Community
- Lifelong Learning
- Celebrating Success

At each level, these themes are narrowed to subthemes that are level-appropriate in content and language.

English—No Problem! Series Components

Five levels make up the series:
- literacy
- level 1 (low beginning)
- level 2 (high beginning)
- level 3 (low intermediate)
- level 4 (high intermediate)

The series includes the following components.

Student Book

A full-color student book is the core of each level of *English—No Problem!* Literacy skills, vocabulary, grammar, reading, writing, listening, speaking, and SCANS-type skills are taught and practiced.

Teacher's Edition

Each teacher's edition includes these tools:
- general suggestions for using the series
- scope and sequence charts for the level
- lesson-specific teacher notes with reduced student book pages
- complete scripts for all listening activities and Pronunciation Targets in the student book

Workbook

A workbook provides contextualized practice in the skills taught at each level. Activities relate to the student book stories. Workbook activities are especially useful for learners working individually.

 This icon in the teacher's edition indicates where workbook activities can be assigned.

Reproducible Masters

The reproducible masters include photocopiable materials for the level. Some masters are unit-specific, such as contextualized vocabulary and grammar activities, games, and activities focusing on higher-level thinking skills. Others are generic graphic organizers. Still other masters can be used by teachers, peers, and learners themselves to assess the work done in each unit.

Each masters book also includes scripts for all listening activities in the masters. (Note: These activities are *not* included on the *English—No Problem!* audio recordings.)

 This icon in the teacher's edition indicates where reproducible masters can be used.

Audio Recording

Available on CD and cassette, each level's audio component includes listening passages, listening activities, and Pronunciation Targets from the student book.

This icon in the student book and teacher's edition indicates that the audio recording includes material for that activity.

Lesson-Plan Builder

This free, web-based *Lesson-Plan Builder* allows teachers to create and save customized lesson plans, related graphic organizers, and selected assessment masters. Goals, vocabulary lists, and other elements are already in the template for each lesson. Teachers then add their own notes to customize their plans. They can also create original graphic organizers using generic templates.

When a lesson plan is finished, the customized materials can be printed and stored in PDF form.

This icon in the teacher's edition refers teachers to the *Lesson-Plan Builder,* found at www.enp.newreaderspress.com.

Vocabulary Cards

For literacy, level 1, and level 2, all vocabulary from the Picture Dictionaries and Vocabulary boxes in the student books is also presented on reproducible flash cards. At the literacy level, the cards also include capital letters, lowercase letters, and numerals.

Placement Tool

The Placement Test student booklet includes items that measure exit skills for each level of the series so that learners can start work in the appropriate student book. The teacher's guide includes a listening script, as well as guidelines for administering the test to a group, for giving an optional oral test, and for interpreting scores.

Hot Topics in ESL

These online professional development articles by adult ESL experts focus on key issues and instructional techniques embodied in *English—No Problem!,* providing background information to enhance effective use of the materials. They are available online at www.enp.newreaderspress.com.

Addressing the Standards

English—No Problem! has been correlated from the earliest stages of development with national standards for adult education and ESL, including the NRS (National Reporting System), EFF (Equipped for the Future), SCANS (Secretary's Commission on Achieving Necessary Skills), CASAS (Comprehensive Adult Student Assessment System) competencies, BEST (Basic English Skills Test), and SPLs (Student Performance Levels). The series also reflects state standards from New York, California, and Florida.

About the Student Books

Each unit in the student books includes a two-page unit opener followed by three lessons (two at the literacy level). A cumulative unit project concludes each unit. Every unit addresses all four language skills—

listening, speaking, reading, and writing. Each lesson focuses on characters operating in one of the three EFF-defined adult roles—parent/family member at home, worker at school or work, or citizen/community member in the larger community.

Unit Opener Pages

Unit Goals The vocabulary, language, pronunciation, and culture goals set forth in the unit opener correlate to a variety of state and national standards.

Opening Question and Photo The opening question, photo, and caption introduce the unit protagonists and engage learners affectively in issues the unit explores.

Think and Talk This feature of levels 1–4 presents questions based on classic steps in problem-posing methodology, adjusted and simplified as needed.

What's Your Opinion? In levels 1–4, this deliberately controversial question often appears after Think and Talk or on the first page of a lesson. It is designed to encourage lively teacher-directed discussion, even among learners with limited vocabulary.

Picture Dictionary or Vocabulary Box This feature introduces important unit vocabulary and concepts.

Gather Your Thoughts In levels 1–4, this activity helps learners relate the unit theme to their own lives. They record their thoughts in a graphic organizer, following a model provided.

What's the Problem? This activity, which follows Gather Your Thoughts, encourages learners to practice another step in problem posing. They identify a possible problem and apply the issue to their own lives.

Setting Goals This feature of levels 1–4 is the first step of a unit's self-evaluation strand. Learners choose from a list of language and life goals and add their own goal to the list. The goals are related to the lesson activities and tasks and to the unit project. After completing a unit, learners revisit these goals in Check Your Progress, the last page of each workbook unit.

First Lesson Page

While the unit opener sets up an issue or problem, the lessons involve learners in seeking solutions while simultaneously developing language competencies.

Lesson Goals and EFF Role The lesson opener lists language, culture, and life-skill goals and identifies the EFF role depicted in that lesson.

Pre-Reading or Pre-Listening Question This question prepares learners to seek solutions to the issues presented in the reading or listening passage or lesson graphic that follows.

Reading or Listening Tip At levels 1–4, this feature presents comprehension and analysis strategies used by good listeners and readers.

Lesson Stimulus Each lesson starts with a reading passage (a picture story at the literacy level), a listening passage, or a lesson graphic. A photo on the page sets the situation for a listening passage. Each listening passage is included in the audio recording, and scripts are provided at the end of the student book and the teacher's edition. A lesson graphic may be a schedule, chart, diagram, graph, time line, or similar item. The questions that follow each lesson stimulus focus on comprehension and analysis.

Remaining Lesson Pages

Picture Dictionary, Vocabulary Box, and Idiom Watch These features present the active lesson vocabulary. At lower levels, pictures often help convey meaning. Vocabulary boxes for the literacy level also include letters and numbers. At levels 3 and 4, idioms are included in every unit.

Class, Group, or Partner Chat This interactive feature provides a model miniconversation. The model sets up a real-life exchange that encourages use of the lesson vocabulary and grammatical structures. Learners ask highly structured and controlled questions and record classmates' responses in a graphic organizer.

Grammar Talk At levels 1–4, the target grammatical structure is presented in several examples. Following the examples is a short explanation or question that guides learners to come up with a rule on their own. At the literacy level, language boxes highlight basic grammatical structures without formal teaching.

Pronunciation Target In this feature of levels 1–4, learners answer questions that lead them to discover pronunciation rules for themselves.

Chat Follow-Ups Learners use information they recorded during the Chat activity. They write patterned sentences, using lesson vocabulary and structures.

In the US This feature is a short cultural reading or brief explanation of some aspect of US culture.

Compare Cultures At levels 1–4, this follow-up to In the US asks learners to compare the custom or situation in the US to similar ones in their home countries.

Activities A, B, C, etc. These practice activities, most of them interactive, apply what has been learned in the lesson so far.

Lesson Tasks Each lesson concludes with a task that encourages learners to apply the skills taught and practiced earlier. Many tasks involve pair or group work, as well as follow-up presentations to the class.

Challenge Reading

At level 4, a two-page reading follows the lessons. This feature helps learners develop skills that prepare them for longer readings they will encounter in future study or higher-level jobs.

Unit Project

Each unit concludes with a final project in which learners apply all or many of the skills they acquired in the unit. The project consists of carefully structured and sequenced individual, pair, and group activities. These projects also help develop important higher-level skills such as planning, organizing, collaborating, and presenting.

Additional Features

The following minifeatures appear as needed at different levels:

One Step Up These extensions of an activity, task, or unit project allow learners to work at a slightly higher skill level. This feature is especially useful when classes include learners at multiple levels.

Attention Boxes These unlabeled boxes highlight words and structures that are not taught explicitly in the lesson, but that learners may need. Teachers are encouraged to point out these words and structures and to offer any explanations that learners require.

Remember? These boxes present, in abbreviated form, previously introduced vocabulary and language structures.

Writing Extension This feature encourages learners to do additional writing. It is usually a practical rather than an academic activity.

Technology Extra This extension gives learners guidelines for doing part of an activity, task, or project using such technology as computers, photocopiers, and audio and video recorders.

Contents

Unit 6   Equal Rights **70**

- ◆ Vocabulary: Rights in the workplace • Equality and discrimination
- ◆ Language: Modals: *may, should, could, would* • Present continuous (review) and past continuous
- ◆ Pronunciation: Sounds of *a* • Reductions
- ◆ Culture: Equal rights and the law in the US

Unit 7   Paying Taxes. **82**

- ◆ Vocabulary: Paychecks • Taxes
- ◆ Language: Verbs followed by infinitives • Order of adjectives
- ◆ Pronunciation: Sounds of *e* • Sounds of *t* and *d*
- ◆ Culture: Taxation in the US

Unit 8   Understanding Yourself **94**

- ◆ Vocabulary: Words to describe people • Words to describe relationships
- ◆ Language: Reflexive pronouns • Future with *will* (review) and *going* to
- ◆ Pronunciation: Sounds of *u* • Sounds of *b* and *v*
- ◆ Culture: Marriage in the US

Unit 9   It Takes a Team **106**

- ◆ Vocabulary: Celebrations • Skills for working with other people
- ◆ Language: Direct and indirect object pronouns • Simple past tense of regular and irregular verbs
- ◆ Pronunciation: Sound of the *–tion* ending • Sounds of *r*
- ◆ Culture: Celebrations in the US

Time for a Change

Dealing With Change

Home 1   Community 2   Work/School 3

◆ **Vocabulary** Finding a job • Interviews and applications

◆ **Language** Using *can, cannot,* and *can't* • Present tense of *be* and *have*

◆ **Pronunciation** Sentence stress • Intonation in statements and questions

◆ **Culture** Interviews in the US

Idiom Watch!
dealing with change

HELP WANTED
ELECTRICIAN

How do you feel about change?

This auto company cannot keep all its workers. Nicholas has to change jobs.

Think and Talk

1. What is Nicholas doing? How does he feel?
2. What is his problem?
3. Do you have this problem?
4. Do you know someone who has this problem?

auto = car
keep
wire
electrician

Picture Dictionary   Listen and repeat. Circle new words.

Get meanings from a classmate, your teacher, or a dictionary.
Write the words and their meanings.

application

job

interview

skill

_____
your word

Gather Your Thoughts   Nicholas has a skill. He can work with

wires. Nicholas dreams of becoming an electrician. Do you want to
change jobs? What skills do you have? What kind of work can you do?

affect
dream job
wires

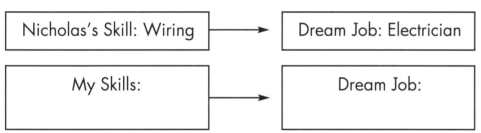

| Nicholas's Skill: Wiring | → | Dream Job: Electrician |

| My Skills: | → | Dream Job: |

What's the Problem?   How do you get the job you want? Do the

changes in your life affect your family and friends? Think about this, or
talk with a partner.

Setting Goals   Think about your answers to the questions above.

What can you do about the problem? Check ✔ your goals.

❏ **1.** List my skills.
❏ **2.** Think about my experience.
❏ **3.** Talk about different jobs with family and friends.
❏ **4.** Learn about job applications.
❏ **5.** Learn about job interviews in the US.
❏ **6.** Another goal: _____

Getting Help

◆ Ask family or friends for help

◆ Use the verbs *can, cannot,* and *can't*

company job training

What do you do when it's time for a change?

◆ **Reading Tip**   One way to understand what you read is to think of your experiences. Think about who can help you make changes. Now read the conversation and answer the questions.

Nicholas:	Elana, I think it's time for me to find a new job. Auto sales are slow. My company cannot keep all the workers. I can't stay there long. But I think that I can get a better job.
Elana:	I know that you can. You helped my Uncle Joe wire his house.
Nicholas:	Yes, I did! That was easy for me.
Elana:	Can you talk to Joe? He's an electrician now. I think he has a very good job.
Nicholas:	But he went to school. I can't stop working to go to school.
Elana:	He worked as an electrician's helper while he went to school. He worked in the mornings and went to school in the afternoons. Also, I can work more to help pay the bills.
Nicholas:	I don't want you to work more hours. Maybe Joe can help me find a job-training program.
Elana:	You can work and get job training at the same time. Then I won't have to work more. Let's talk to Uncle Joe.

It's time for a change.

Talk or Write

1. Why does Nicholas want a different job?
2. What can Nicholas learn from Uncle Joe?
3. Why is a job-training program a good idea?

What's Your Opinion? When you make changes in your life, your family and friends may also need to make changes. Who should you talk to before you make big changes in your life? Why?

Partner Chat Work with a partner. Ask questions. Write answers in your chart.

What can you do?

I can cook.

Me	My Partner
1. *I can cook.*	1.
2.	2.
3.	3.

Grammar Talk: Using *Can*, *Cannot*, and *Can't*

Using *Can*

Nicholas talks to his wife.	Nicholas **can** talk to his wife.
I help my husband think of new ideas.	I **can** help my husband think of new ideas.

Using *Cannot* and *Can't*

I quit my job.	I **cannot** quit my job. OR I **can't** quit my job.
Nicholas stays at his job.	Nicholas **cannot** stay at his job. OR Nicholas **can't** stay at his job.

can   **can't**   **cannot**

What are the two negative forms of can?

Pronunciation Target • Sentence Stress

Listen to your teacher or the audio read the sentences in Grammar Talk. Does your teacher stress can? *Does your teacher stress* can't *and* cannot?

Activity A **Partner Chat Follow-Up** Look at your Partner Chat chart. In your notebook, make new sentences using *can, cannot,* and *can't.*

I can cook. You can fix cars.

Activity B Match the cause to the effect. The *cause* answers the question, "Why?" The *effect* tells what happened. For example, the cause "Auto sales are slow," leads to the effect, "The company can't keep all workers."

Cause	Effect
__b__ **1.** Auto sales are slow.	**a.** Nicholas can learn about a new job.
_____ **2.** Uncle Joe went to school.	**b.** The company can't keep all workers.
_____ **3.** Elana works more hours.	**c.** Uncle Joe is an electrician.
_____ **4.** Nicholas talks to Uncle Joe.	**d.** Nicholas can go to school.

Activity C How can your family and friends help you? Make a chart like this one in your notebook. Write sentences using *can, can't,* and *cannot.* Compare your answers with a partner.

Can	Can't OR Cannot
My sister can help with my children.	My sister cannot give me money.

TASK 1   Make a Job Ladder

Nicholas has a plan to get a better job. A plan like this is called a *job ladder.*

Dream Job: Electrician
Training: Vocational school classes
Entry-Level Job: Electrician's helper
Skills: I can work with my hands. I can work with wires.

Make a job ladder in your notebook. Use Nicholas's job ladder as a model. Start with your skills. Climb up to your dream job.

 Community

Finding Jobs

◆ Find out about job applications

◆ Use simple present tense of *be* and *have* (Review)

What do you need to know to complete a job application?

degree
former
lawfully
recent
references
supervisor

◆ Reading Tip   To read a form, scan the form quickly first to see what it is about. Then read it carefully. Scan the form below. What information does Nicholas need to complete it?

APPLICATION FOR EMPLOYMENT
PLEASE PRINT CLEARLY. COMPLETE ALL ITEMS.

ELECTRO-NOW
Equal Opportunity Employer

PERSONAL INFORMATION

Date: 9/11/04	Social Security number: 999-01-2856	Date of Birth: 12/1/67	Phone: (217) 555-6858

Name: Gorovoy (Last) Nicholas (First) (Middle)	Address: 2122 Elm St. (Street) Springfield (City) IL (State) 61801 (Zip)

Can you lawfully work in the US.? ☑ Yes ☐ No

How do you know about our company? ☐ Walk-in ☐ Newspaper ☐ School ☐ Friend ☐ Agency ☑ Other   a relative

Education	Name and Location	Date
High School	Vladimir, Russia	1981–1985
College	No	
Business, Trade, Other	English Classes	1995–1998

JOB HISTORY
List your last two employers below. Start with your current or last employer.
May we contact your employer? ☑ Yes ☐ No

Employer	Supervisor	Phone Number
General Automotive	Mr. Whitehill	(217) 555-7700
Taxi Drivers R Us	Ms. Roman	(217) 555-2581

Date 9/11/04   Applicant's signature   *Nicholas Gorovoy*

This is a good start.

Talk or Write
1. How old is Nicholas?
2. What is his job now?
3. Did he go to high school?
4. Can he list his employers as references?

Remember?
Social Security number

Class Chat Play Bingo. Walk around and ask, "What are your strengths?" Write the name of a classmate in the correct box. The first person to write a name in every box wins.

I am organized. *Mamie*	I am hard-working.	I am bilingual.
I am on time.	I can learn quickly.	I have many interests.
I have a high school diploma.	I have work experience.	I can teach others.

Vocabulary

Listen and repeat. Circle new words. Get meanings from a classmate, your teacher, or a dictionary. Write the words and their meanings.

degree

reference

supervisor

strength

weakness

bilingual

hard-working

organized

Grammar Talk: Simple Present Tense of *Be* and *Have*

Singular

Be	Have
I **am** happy.	I **have** a good job.
You **are** happy.	You **have** a good job.
He **is** happy.	She **has** a good job.

Plural

We **are** happy.	We **have** good jobs.
They **are** happy.	They **have** good jobs.

Be *and* have *are different from other verbs. Practice the forms now.*

Pronunciation Target • Intonation in Statements and Questions

Listen to your teacher or the audio. Notice when the voice goes up and when it goes down.

Where does Nicholas go for information? ↑

He goes to the Employment Center. ↓

Can you fix things? ↑   Yes, I can. ↓

Activity A Show your job ladder from Task 1 to a school counselor or your teacher. A counselor can help you get to your goal. Get ready to talk. Do these things in your notebook:

- Complete sentences 1 and 2.
- Copy questions 3, 4, and 5. Write answers.
- Write two more things to ask or tell.

1. I can _____ very well.

2. I want to be a (an) _____.

3. What kind of training do I need?

4. Where can I get the training?

5. How long does the training last?

Practice asking and answering with a partner. Then talk to the counselor.

Activity B Employers want to know about your experiences and goals. The chart below shows Nicholas's past experiences and future goals. A plus (+) means it was a good experience for Nicholas. A minus (–) means it was bad. In your notebook, make a chart with your experiences and goals. Use + and – signs. Talk about your chart with a partner. How are your charts the same? How are they different?

Nicholas's Life

Past Experiences
Worked in factory after high school. **–**
Married Elana. **+**
Drove taxi. **–**
Worked for auto company. **+**
Took English classes. **+**

Goals
Become an electrician.

 TASK 2 Write Your Job History

Get a chart like this one from your teacher or make a chart in your notebook. Write your job history. Start with your last job.

Date	Employer's Name	Contact Person	Job Duties
5/98-present	Great Pizza Takeout	Mr. Johnson	Deliver pizza.

contact person = person who can give a reference

Good News!

◆ Learn about job interviews in the US

◆ Prepare for a job interview

| ambitious |
| industry |
| sir |
| start |
| technical |

How can you do well in an interview?

◆ Listening Tip 🎧 Writing difficult words can help you understand what you hear. Listen to the conversation. You can read the words on page 118. Write difficult words in your notebook. Find the words in a dictionary or ask your teacher questions. Then listen again.

Nicholas is at a job interview. The interviewer thinks he can be good for the company.

Talk or Write
1. Where is Nicholas?
2. Why does he want a new job?
3. When can he start?
4. Why is this a good job for Nicholas?

In the US   Preparing for a Job Interview

It is very important to prepare well for a job interview. These ideas can help.

- Wear neat clothes.
- Come on time.
- Be confident and polite.
- Shake hands firmly with the interviewer.
- Make eye contact.
- Never smoke or chew gum.
- Be interested in the job. Ask questions.
- You can ask about pay and benefits. Ask those questions last.
- Thank the interviewer for talking to you.
- Send a short thank-you letter the next day. Ask an English-speaking friend to help you write it.

☛ Compare Cultures

What do you do in your country to prepare for a job interview?

- Talk with a partner about your country.
- Draw circles like these to compare your country to the US.
- Tell the class about your country.

Vocabulary

Listen and repeat. Circle new words. Get meanings from a classmate, your teacher, or a dictionary. Write the words and their meanings.

benefits

company

eye contact

interviewer

pay

ambitious

confident

interested (in)

neat

polite

_____
your word

prepare = get ready for
   shake hands
   smoke
   chew gum

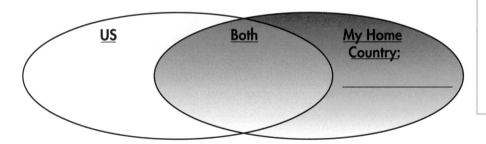

US   Both   My Home Country: _____

Activity A   Look at the picture on page 18. Then read In the US again. Decide on the five most important things to do in an interview. Write them in your notebook. Number them from one to five. Write the most important thing on line 1. Then work with your group. Tally the rankings. Make a final group list of the five most important things to do to in an interview.

Activity B   Look at catalogs and magazines. Cut out pictures of people dressed for your dream job. Make a class poster with the pictures. Write your name, your skills, and your dream job under the picture you selected. Hang your poster in the classroom.

Activity C   With a small group, role-play a really bad interview. Look at the list of things to do in In the US. Try to do everything wrong. You can talk a lot or you can talk very little. Let the class select the worst interview and explain why it is the worst.

Activity D   Work in a group. Play Give One, Get One:
- Each group member writes one question to ask in an interview.
- Send a group member to other groups to give a question to and get a question from each group.
- Write a list of questions in your group.
- Write all the questions in your notebook.

1. What are the work hours?

One Step Up
Use the class poster to tell the class about your dream job. Say these things:
My name is

_____.

I can

_____.

I have a dream job. It is

_____.

I think I will be successful because I am

_____.

TASK 3   Talk about Your Strengths
Read the list below. Check your strengths. With a partner, give examples of your strengths.

strengths = things that you do well

_____ am organized   _____ am hard-working
_____ can teach skills   _____ have many interests
_____ speak two languages   _____ can learn fast
_____ come to work on time   _____ _____
_____ have job experience   (another strength)

In a chart like this one, write how you use the skills. Think carefully about your strengths. You don't have to write something about every skill in every column.

Skills	Family	Work	School	Community
I am organized.	I help my children get to school on time.			

Complete an Application Form

Sometimes companies and schools want you to complete an application form at the interview. It can help to have an information form ready.

Get Ready

Complete this information form. Bring it with you to job interviews or school interviews.

P E R S O N A L :

Name: _____   Date of Birth: _____

Address: _____   Phone: _____

Emergency Contact: _____   Phone: _____

W O R K   E X P E R I E N C E : (List last job first.)

Dates	**Company**	**Contact Person**
_____	_____	_____
_____	_____	_____

E D U C A T I O N / T R A I N I N G :

High School: _____

Dates: _____

Technical School: _____

Dates: _____

Higher Education: _____

Dates: _____

Do the Work

Get the application form from your teacher. Complete the application. Use the information that you wrote in Get Ready.

Present Your Project

Have an interview party with your class. Practice interviewing for your dream job with your teacher or a counselor. Dress correctly to interview for this job. Use your information form to talk about your strengths. Explain why your strengths are important for this job.

Writing Extension   In your notebook, write about your dream job. What is most exciting about the job? What seems most difficult? Why?

🖥 Technology Extra

Use a computer to type your basic information worksheet. Or use the Internet to look for your dream job. Can you find the average salary?

New Beginnings

Coming Together

Home
1

Work/School
2

Community
3

◆ **Vocabulary** Moving and feelings • Activities • Volunteer jobs • Places to volunteer • Immigration

◆ **Language** Simple past tense of regular verbs • Simple past tense of irregular verbs

◆ **Pronunciation** Sounds of simple past-tense endings • Sounds of *o*

◆ **Culture** Measurements in the US

Fotini is excited about her new life in the US.

How do you contribute to your family and your community?

Think and Talk

1. Where is Fotini?
2. What is she thinking? What is she feeling?
3. How did you feel when you came to the US?

Picture Dictionary Listen and repeat. Circle new words.
Get meanings from a classmate, your teacher, or a dictionary.
Write the words and their meanings.

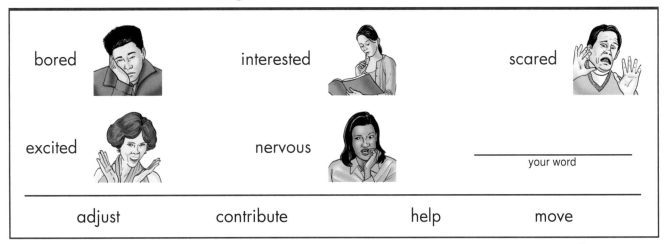

bored

interested

scared

excited

nervous

_____
your word

_____

adjust   contribute   help   move

Gather Your Thoughts How did you feel when you came to the
US? Make an idea map with your teacher. Add feeling words. Write +
if the feeling was good. Write – if the feeling was bad. Then make an
idea map like this one in your notebook.

Idiom Watch!
call home
make friends

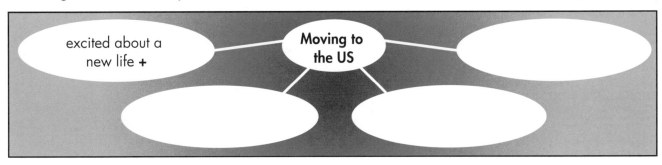

excited about a
new life +

Moving to
the US

What's the Problem? Moving to the US is a big change. Many
people feel excited and scared. How did you adjust to the United States?
Think about this, or talk with a partner.

Setting Goals Think about your answers to the questions above.
What can you do about the problem? Check ✔ your goals.

❑ **1.** Learn new skills.
❑ **2.** Make new friends.
❑ **3.** Teach new skills.

❑ **4.** Learn about my community.
❑ **5.** Help others.
❑ **6.** Another goal: _____

Adjusting to a New Country

◆ Talk about daily actions and skills

◆ Take a phone message

◆ Use simple past tense (Review)

Is listening to phone messages difficult for you? Why?

◆ Listening Tip 🎧 One way to understand a phone message is to save the message and listen again. It is also good to take notes. Now you will hear a phone message. Get ready to write notes. You will need a pen and paper. First listen to the message. Don't write. Listen again. Take notes. Answer these questions. Check your answers with a partner. You can read the words on page 118.

> I hope I can understand this message.

Fotini wants to understand the message. Then she can tell her daughter about it.

Talk or Write

1. Who called?
2. What did she want?
3. Where are the sisters?

Picture Dictionary   Listen and repeat. Circle new words.
Get meanings from a classmate, your teacher, or a dictionary.
Write the words and their meanings.

call   cook   shop wait,

call   cook   shop   wash

clean    play   walk   _____
                                                          your word

Class Chat   Look at the Picture Dictionary above. Role-play
a word for the class. The class will guess the word. Write the
words in a chart like this one in your notebook.

I go to a store.

She shops.

Name	What's Happening?	What Happened?
Marta	She shops.	She shopped.

Grammar Talk: Simple Past Tense of Regular Verbs

Simple Present:	I talk on the phone.	Marta talks on the phone.
Simple Past:	I talk**ed** on the phone.	Marta talk**ed** on the phone.

call	called	clean	cleaned	cook	cooked	play	played
shop	shopped	talk	talked	walk	walked	wash	washed

How do you make the simple past? Remember: verb + ed = simple past.

Pronunciation Target • Sounds of Simple Past Tense Endings

🎧 *Listen to your teacher or the audio. Do you hear the difference between the sounds of -ed?*

d sound	*id* sound	*t* sound
called	wanted	cooked
cleaned	added	talked

Activity A   **Class Chat Follow-Up** Look at your Class Chat chart.
In your notebook, write sentences about your classmates.

<u>Marta talks on the phone. Marta talked on the phone.</u>

Activity B   Work with a partner. Leave a message, and listen to a
message. Do these things:

1. Partner A: Write a note, call a friend, and leave a message
to invite the friend to dinner.
2. Partner B: Listen to the message, and take notes.
3. Partner B: Leave a message. Partner A: take notes.

When you leave a message, say these things:

- Your name: _____

- Why you called: _____

  _____

- Call back? _____

  _____

- Your phone number: _____

When you take notes, write these things:

> **IMPORTANT MESSAGE**
>
> Name of caller: _____
>
> Message: _____
>
> _____
>
> Call back?   Yes   No
>
> Phone Number: _____

Activity C   Listen to Fotini and her daughter Ritza talk. Ritza
wants to help Fotini adjust. Work with a partner. Write an ending for
their conversation.

TASK 1 List Your Skills

Make a chart like this one. Write all your special skills. How can you
use your skills with your family, at work, and in your community?

Skills	Family and Friends	Work	Community
Cook	Teach the children to cook.	Give recipes to people at work.	Bring cakes to church.

Giving and Learning

◆ Talk about helping in your community

◆ Use simple past tense of irregular verbs

craft
dessert
festival
a lot
sale
set up
sign up
volunteer

How do you contribute at work, at school, or in your community?

◆ Reading Tip *Scanning* is reading quickly for important information. Look at the big words in a flyer or a form first. It tells the important things. Then read the small words for details. Now scan this flyer and answer the questions.

WASHINGTON SCHOOL

Fall Festival

Saturday, 11/10
9:00 a.m. – 12:00 noon

Games
Crafts
Food
Bake Sale

Everyone Can Come!

VOLUNTEER TO HELP! SIGN UP!

Name: *Fotini Papas*

Guests: *Ritza, Raisa, Luisa*

Sell tickets: _____

Set up and clean up: _____

Help with games: _____

Help with crafts: _____

Bring food for bake sale: ___

Sell food and drinks: _____

Sorry, I can't help: _____

Thank you!

When everyone helps a little, a lot can happen. Fotini helped at the school festival. She baked a Greek dessert for the bake sale.

Talk or Write
1. Where is the festival? When is it?
2. How does Fotini help?
3. What happens at the fall festival?
4. Who can come?

Class Chat   Your teacher will give you a volunteer job. Remember your job. Do these things:

- Put the chairs in a circle.
- One person stands in the center and asks, "How do you help at _____?" (a place to volunteer)
- If your volunteer job matches the place, stand, answer the question, and change places with the person in the center.
- The last person stands, reads a volunteer job, and starts the game again.

How do you help at the hospital?

I visit sick people.

Vocabulary

Listen and repeat. Circle new words. Get meanings from a classmate, your teacher, or a dictionary. Write the words and their meanings.

bring a meal to
  a busy friend

build homes

clean up

sell tickets

serve meals

teach crafts

visit sick people

volunteer

church festival

community

homeless shelter

hospital

local park

neighborhood

school

Grammar Talk: Simple Past Tense of Irregular Verbs

bring	brought	Fotini **brought** dessert to the festival.
build	built	We **built** homes for poor people.
come	came	Fotini **came** to the US to help Ritza.
go	went	The girls **went** to clean up the park.
leave	left	She **left** her home for a new life.
feel	felt	Dusan **felt** confident about his job.
make	made	Who **made** this beautiful cake?
sell	sold	Fotini **sold** her home in Greece.
sing	sang	In Bosnia, I **sang** in school.
sit	sat	We **sat** in a circle.
take	took	They **took** their dog to the park every day last summer.
teach	taught	Ritza **taught** her daughters English and Greek.

The simple past tense of irregular verbs doesn't end in -ed. You have to memorize each form. Practice with a partner. Read the sentences. Then listen to your partner read them. Can you guess what other verbs are irregular? For more irregular verbs, see page 125.

Pronunciation Target • Sounds of o

🎧 *Listen to your teacher or the audio.*

Short *o*	Long *o*	Long *o*	Long *o*
shop	phone	road	low
got	broke	coach	throw

*The letter **o** has different sounds in English. Copy this chart in your notebook.*

Activity A **Class Chat Follow-Up** Use the sentences from the Class Chat. Write sentences in the simple past tense. Put a check ✔ by the irregular verbs.

How did you help at the hospital? I visited sick people.

One Step Up
Role-play something you did yesterday. The class can guess what you did.

Activity B Look at the volunteer flyer on page 27. Write things that volunteers did at the school festival. Use the past tense.

1. *They sold tickets.*

2. _____

3. _____

4. _____

Activity C Think about these ways to help in your community. Write two more ways in your notebook. Check the most interesting thing to do.

international
invite
service

- Clean up a public place.
- Walk in a walk-a-thon.
- Start a baby-sitting service with other parents.
- Organize an international party and invite friends and family.

TASK 2 Make a Poster for a Class Party

Work with your class. Design a poster or a flyer for an international class party. Write these things on the poster: what the party is for, where the party is, what day and time the party is, and who to talk to about the party.

Sharing Cultures in the US

- ◆ Learn about the history of immigration to the US
- ◆ Calculate liquid and solid measurements

adventure

recipe

Why did you come to the US?

- ◆ Reading Tip   You need to know some special vocabulary when you read history. Use the context, or the words around it, to help you understand a new word. Read about immigration below. What new words do you need to learn?

Immigration

People from many countries come to the US for many different reasons. Immigrants are an important part of the history of the US. Some immigrants come for political reasons. Their ideas are not popular with their governments. Some come for economic reasons. They want the opportunity to make money so their families can live better lives. Some come for personal reasons. They want to join their families or find adventure.

Immigrants contribute many things to their new communities. They bring with them new ideas and many skills. They help their families and friends. They share their cultures. As part of those cultures, they bring their recipes! Many popular foods in the US are from other countries. It is not easy to name a true American food. Think about it: Do *hamburgers* and *french fries* really sound American?

Talk or Write
1. What sentence helps you know what *political* means?
2. What does *economic* mean?
3. What is an example of a personal reason for coming to the US?

In the US   Measurements

People in the US use a different measurement system than most of the world. Immigrants may need to change, or convert, metric measurements to the US system.

Multiply	By	To Convert To
liters	.264	gallons
liters	1.057	quarts
liters	4.228	cups
grams	.035	ounces
kilograms (kilos)	2.205	pounds

> convert = change

☛ Compare Cultures

Compare foods you ate in your home country with foods you eat in the United States.

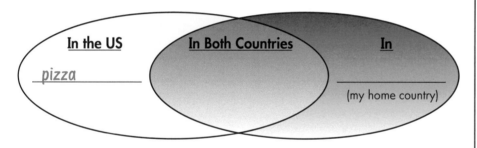

In the US

pizza

In Both Countries

In _____

(my home country)

Talk in a group. What did you like about food in your home country? What do you like about food in the United States?

Activity A   In your notebook, write the "Immigration" reading from page 30 in the past tense.

People from many countries came to the United States for many different reasons.

Vocabulary

Listen and repeat. Circle new words. Get meanings from a classmate, your teacher, or a dictionary. Write the words and their meanings.

history

immigrant

immigration

economic

personal

political

culture

government

popular

_____

your word

One Step Up
Think of a recipe from your country to share at the class party. Convert the recipe to US measurements. Bring it to class for the project at the end of this unit.

Activity B With your group, tell why you came to the US. In your notebook, make a chart for your group.

Date	Name	Reason for Coming to US
1. 1999	Ming Wu	to get married
2.		

One Step Up
Do you know a famous immigrant from your home country? Tell the class about that person.

Activity C Talk in a group of four or five students. Talk about music or dances from your home countries and other countries. Complete a chart in your notebook.

	Country	Music or Dance	Food
1.	Brazil	Samba	Feijoada
2.			
3.			
4.			
5.			

Activity D Fotini still makes her shopping lists with the metric system. Raisa and Luisa want her to understand US measurements. Can you complete these conversions?

shopping list

1 liter of milk = _____ gallons of milk

3 kilos of potatoes = _____ pounds of potatoes

300 grams of cheese = _____ ounces of cheese

TASK 3 Sharing Your Culture

Write the words to a famous song from your country or bring a recording of the song to class. Tell the class about the song. What do you know about the song's history?

One Step Up
Teach the song to the class.

famous
recording

Plan an International Party

Plan an international celebration for your class.

Get Ready

In small groups, with other people from your home country, plan a celebration. Is it difficult for your class to have a party now? Select a date later in the school year, maybe before a vacation or at the end of school. Write things that each member of the group can contribute. Make a chart like this one.

celebration = party

Contribution	Describe	Name and Home Country
Food and recipe	empanadas (turnovers)	Felicia Gomez—Peru
Song or dance		
Photos with words		
Books and magazines		
Crafts		
Drinks/sodas		

Do the Work

1. Meet every week with your group to talk about the party plans. Use the chart from your teacher to make a time line.
2. Write recipes on the form your teacher gives you. Collect the class recipes and collect the songs from Task 3 (page 32).
3. Make a class book of recipes and songs from your home countries.
4. One or two students can volunteer to make a cover for the book.

Present Your Project

At the party, tell the class about what you contributed to the party.

Writing Extension Write your project presentation in your notebook.

📱 Technology Extra

Leave a phone message for your teacher at your school. Tell what you liked best about the class party.

Balancing Your Life

Finding Balance

Work/School   Community   Home
1   2   3

- **Vocabulary** Responsibilities and feelings • Health • Sports and leisure activities
- **Language** Compound sentences with *and* or *but* • *Do* and *does* in Yes/No questions and answers
- **Pronunciation** Pauses and intonation in compound sentences • Sounds of *i*
- **Culture** Being too busy

Is your life balanced?   Silvia Lopez feels tired, stressed, and sick.

Think and Talk

1. What is Silvia doing?
2. What is her problem?
3. Who is helping Silvia?
4. What does she want to do?
5. Do you ever feel like this?

Picture Dictionary   Listen and repeat. Circle new words.
Get meanings from a classmate, your teacher, or a dictionary.
Write the words and their meanings.

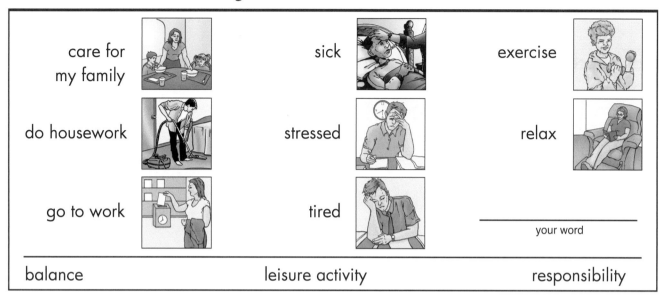

care for
my family

do housework

go to work

sick

stressed

tired

exercise

relax

_____
your word

balance   leisure activity   responsibility

Gather Your Thoughts   How do you feel about your responsibilities
and leisure activities? Make an idea map like this one.

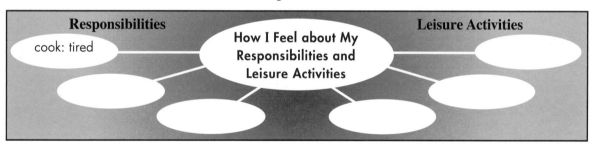

Responsibilities   **Leisure Activities**

cook: tired

How I Feel about My
Responsibilities and
Leisure Activities

Talk with a partner. Can some responsibilities be fun? Explain.

What's the Problem?   Do you have more responsibilities or
more leisure activities? Is there an activity you want to do but can't?
Why can't you? Think about this or talk with a partner.

Remember?

happy

sad

Setting Goals   Think about your answers to the questions above.
What can you do about the problem? Check ✔ your goals.

❑ **1.** Plan my time better.
❑ **2.** Ask for changes in my job.
❑ **3.** Find a new activity.
❑ **4.** Talk to a doctor.

❑ **5.** Talk to a friend.
❑ **6.** Learn to ask for help with my responsibilities.
❑ **7.** Another goal: _____

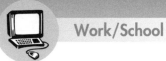

Too Much Work!

◆ Talk about your responsibilities

◆ Use compound sentences with *and* or *but*

| laundry room |
| nursing home |
| schedule |

How much work is too much work?

◆ Reading Tip Learning to read schedules well is important. Now look at the schedule below. When does Silvia work?

Restful Nursing Home
Laundry Room Work Schedule

	S	M	T	W	TH	F	S
Silvia (Wash/dry)	6:00 a.m.–12:00 noon	6:00 a.m.–2:00 p.m.	6:00 a.m.–2:00 p.m.	6:00 a.m.–2:00 p.m.	6:00 a.m.–12:00 noon	6:00 a.m.–12:00 noon	
José (Fold/sort)		8:00 a.m.–4:00 p.m.	8:00 a.m.–4:00 p.m.	8:00 a.m.–4:00 p.m.	8:00 a.m.–4:00 p.m.	8:00 a.m.–2:00 p.m.	8:00 a.m.–2:00 p.m.
Julia (Wash/dry)	12:00 noon–6:00 p.m.	12:00 noon–8:00 p.m.	12:00 noon–8:00 p.m.	12:00 noon–8:00 p.m.	12:00 noon–6:00 p.m.		
Susan (Fold/sort)	8:00 a.m.–4:00 p.m.	8:00 a.m.–2:00 p.m.	8:00 a.m.–2:00 p.m.	8:00 a.m.–4:00 p.m.	8:00 a.m.–4:00 p.m.		
Miguel (Iron/deliver to rooms)	8:00 a.m.–4:00 p.m.	8:00 a.m.–4:00 p.m.	8:00 a.m.–4:00 p.m.	8:00 a.m.–2:00 p.m.			

I feel sick, but I have to go to work.

Talk or Write

1. How many people work in the laundry room?
2. What do workers do in the laundry room?
3. When does Silvia work? How many hours does she work each week?

Picture Dictionary   Listen or repeat. Circle new words.
Get meanings from a classmate, your teacher, or a dictionary.
Write the words and their meanings.

baby-sit	drive	office	time off
call in sick	hours	study	_____ your word

Class Chat   Walk around. Ask questions.
Write the answers.

What do you do?   I work in a laundry room.

What's your name?	What do you do?	What else do you do?
Miroslav	I work in a laundry room.	I play the guitar.

Grammar Talk: Compound Sentences with *And* or *But*

Two sentences:	Kattia baby-sits. She studies English.
Compound sentence:	Kattia baby-sits, **and** she studies English.
Two sentences:	Juan drives a bus. Dora drives a bus.
Compound sentence:	Juan drives a bus, **and** Dora **does too.**
Two sentences:	Raul wants to play guitar. He doesn't have time.
Compound sentence:	Raul wants to play guitar, **but** he doesn't have time.

Put two sentences together with and *or* but. *Use commas.*

Pronunciation Target • Pauses and Intonation in Compound Sentences

🎧 *Listen to your teacher or the audio. Does the voice stop between the two parts of the sentence? Does the voice rise on the word before the comma?*

Charles is a mechanic, and Maria is too. She feels tired, but she has to clean the house.

Activity A **Class Chat Follow-Up** Use your Class Chat chart to write sentences in your notebook.

Miroslav works in a laundry room, and he plays the guitar.

Activity B Talk to a partner about one thing that you want to do and why you can't do it. Remember to pause in the middle of the sentence. Then listen to your partner, and write about your partner.

I want to swim, but I don't have time.

I want to visit my parents in Korea, but I have to work.

Activity C Silvia writes a note to her boss. She asks for a change in her work schedule. Work with a partner to complete the note. Use the words in the box.

| five |
| work |
| take care |
| schedule |
| 12:00 |
| study |

October 5, 2004
Dear Mr. Riley:

    Can you change my _____?
I like my work at Restful Nursing Home, but I want to work

only _____ days a week, from 6:00 to

_____. I need to _____

less because I also have to _____ English

and _____ of my family.
Can we talk soon?
Sincerely,
Silvia Lopez

TASK 1 Explain a Schedule Change

Write a note to your boss. Ask for a change in your schedule. Maybe you want to work longer hours one day a week and not work on Sunday. Maybe you want to work more hours to get more money. Use Silvia's note as a model. If you don't work, write a note to your teacher. Explain why you have to miss class.

One Step Up
With a partner, role-play a conversation. One partner is a boss. The other partner is a worker. The worker wants to work a different schedule.

 Community

Stressed!

◆ Talk about health problems and feelings

◆ Use *do* and *does* in Yes/No questions and answers

infection
prescription

How do you feel when you work too much?

◆ Listening Tip 🎧 When you listen, think about what you want to learn. This is your *listening focus.* Now listen to the conversation between Silvia and her doctor. Listen carefully for Silvia's symptoms. You can read the words on page 118.

Silvia knows she needs help. She talks to her doctor.

Talk or Write
1. Where is Silvia?
2. Why does the doctor give Silvia a prescription?
3. Why does the doctor tell Silvia to relax?

What's Your Opinion? Will Silvia ask her family for help? Explain.

Pronunciation Target • Sounds of *i*

🎧 *The letter* i *has different sounds in English. Listen to your teacher or the audio say* tired, life, *and* night. *These words have a long* i *sound.*

Next listen to the words sick *and* swim. *These words have a short* i *sound.*

Think of other words with these sounds. Write the words on cards. Practice with a partner. Say your words and your partner's words.

Vocabulary

Listen and repeat. Circle new words. Get meanings from a classmate, your teacher, or a dictionary. Write the words and their meanings.

headache

sore throat

stomachache

symptom

antibiotic

pharmacy

pill

prescription

_____
your word

Class Chat   Walk around. Ask questions with these words:

fever   headache   sore throat   stomachache

Write answers in your chart.

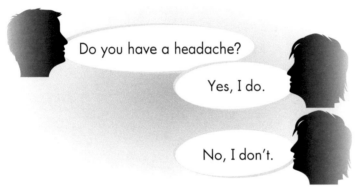

Do you have a headache?

Yes, I do.

No, I don't.

What's your name?	Do you feel sick?	What's your problem?
Silvia Lopez	Yes, I do.	I have a headache.

Grammar Talk: *Do* and *Does* in Yes/No Questions and Answers

Do I need more sleep?	Yes, you **do.**	OR	No, you **don't.**
Do you have a stomachache?	Yes, I **do.**	OR	No, I **don't.**
Does Silvia have a sore throat?	Yes, she **does.**	OR	No, she **doesn't.**
Do we go to work now?	Yes, we **do.**	OR	No, we **don't.**
Do they have class tonight?	Yes, they **do.**	OR	No, they **don't.**

When do you use does? *Can you give a long answer for each question?*

Activity A **Class Chat Follow-Up** Use the answers from the Class Chat to write questions and answers with *do* and *does*.

<u>*Does Carmelo have a headache? Yes, he does.*</u>

Activity B Look at the pie chart. It tells what Silvia does on Mondays. With a partner, ask and answer questions. Write the answers.

On Mondays, how many hours does Silvia work at her job?

She works at her job 8 hours.

Pie chart:
- 1 hr. Clean
- 1 hr. Drive
- 6 hrs. Sleep
- 2 hrs. Study English
- 2 hrs. Children's homework & activities
- 2 hrs. Get self & children ready
- 2 hrs. Cook meals
- 8 hrs. Work at job

With your partner, read and answer the questions.

1. How many hours does Silvia have to relax?
2. Does Silvia balance her life? Why or why not?

Activity C Make a pie chart for a workday. Write all the things that you do.

Activity D Read Silvia's notes for her talk with the doctor.

> Most days I work at my job for 8 hours, and I sleep for 6 hours. I get the children ready for school, and I get myself ready for work. That takes 2 hours. I cook for 2 hours, and I study English for 2 hours. I clean for 1 hour, and I drive for 1 hour. I spend 1 hour at my children's activities, and I help them with homework for 1 hour. I do all these things, but I don't have time for leisure activities. Next week, I will cook for only 1 hour. Then I will play tennis with a friend.

Write about your life in your notebook. Use your pie chart for ideas. Use Silvia's notes as a model.

 TASK 2 Chart Your Activities

Make a chart with your activities for one week.

Day	Date	Paid Work	School	Work at Home	Leisure Activities
M	4/2	8 hours	3 hours	do housework - 1 hour	watch TV - 45 minutes

Work and Play

◆ Talk about sports and hobbies

◆ Learn about how busy life in the US can be

| gym |
| sign up |

What do your children do after school?

◆ Reading Tip   Pictures can help you guess, or predict, what a reading is about. When you read, check your guesses, or predictions, to see if they were correct. Now look at the picture before you read. Can you predict what Silvia is reading?

Dear Ms. Lopez:

Your daughter, Selena, is doing well in gym class. She is an excellent team player. Soccer starts next week. Will she sign up for the team? Registration is Monday after school in the school gym. Practice is every Monday, Wednesday, and Friday from 3 to 5. Please call me if you have any questions.

Sincerely,

Ruth Bradley

Gym Teacher

Talk or Write

1. What does the teacher want Selena to do?
2. How do you think Silvia feels? Why?

What's Your Opinion? Should Silvia let Selena join the team? Why or why not?

Picture Dictionary

Listen and repeat. Circle new words.
Get meanings from a classmate, your teacher, or a dictionary.
Write the words and their meanings.

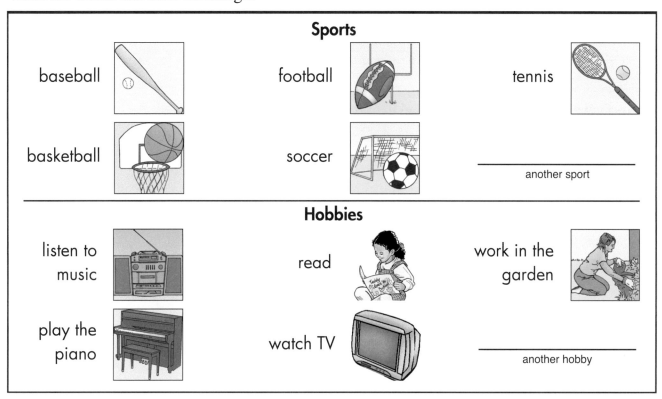

Sports

baseball

football

tennis

basketball

soccer

_____
another sport

Hobbies

listen to
music

read

work in the
garden

play the
piano

watch TV

_____
another hobby

★ In the US   How Busy Is Too Busy?

Does it seem like everyone is busy? People are very active. Many women work outside the home, and they take care of their families too. Many men work long hours, but they also want time with their children. Children have homework, sports, and other activities after school. Everyone is busy all the time! Many people say they are stressed. They want to slow down, but they don't or they can't.

Activity A   Write the names of five popular leisure activities in your home country. Tell a small group about leisure activities in your country and in the US.

☞ Compare Cultures

Was life busy in your home country, or was it relaxed? Talk with a partner. Then share your ideas with the class.

active

Soccer is really popular in Bolivia, and it is popular in the US too.

Chess is popular in Romania, but it's not very popular in the US.

Activity B Talk with three people in the class. Ask about their leisure activities.

What do you do to relax?

I play soccer.

What else do you do?

I watch TV.

Write answers in your notebook. Read them to the class.

<u>Gloria watches TV, and she plays soccer.</u>

else

Activity C Silvia's doctor listened to Silvia talk about her problems. Silvia and her family also need to talk about their problems. When people talk without getting stressed or angry, they can understand and solve problems.

As a class, read the questions. Talk about other questions that Silvia and her family can ask. In groups, role-play the conversations. Talk about solutions to the problems.

1. How can Silvia's husband help her? He can ask: "Why do you feel tired and sad?"
2. How can Silvia help Selena? She can ask: "Do you really want to play soccer?"
3. How can the children help? They can ask: "Can we help do the housework?"

 TASK 3 Find Community Activities

What sports and other leisure activities does your community have? Work with a small group. Look at some of these things in class:

- newspapers and flyers
- phone books
- cable TV
- the Internet
- information from community centers and libraries

Bring flyers to class. Put them on the bulletin board. In a chart, write five sports or leisure activities that people in your group are interested in.

A Presentation about Your Life

Prepare a class presentation about you and your life.

Get Ready

Get five note cards from your teacher. On each card write about one of these things:

photo = photograph

1. Everything you do during one week
2. Your job (if you have one) or family responsibilities
   - where you work
   - what you do
   - your work schedule
3. What you like to do and why it is important to you
   - a food that you cook
   - a musical instrument that you play
   - a favorite sport or hobby
4. How you feel at different times of the week
   - what you like to do and why
   - what you don't like to do and why
5. What you will do to balance your life
   - what you want to do this year to balance your life
   - how you plan to reach that goal

Find a photo that shows an important part of your life.

Do the Work

Read your notes several times. Practice presenting alone. Then practice with a friend. Make eye contact. Speak in a loud voice. Speak slowly. Ask for suggestions. Practice again . . . and again.

Present Your Project

Tell the class about your life. Use your cards and your photo.

Writing Extension Choose one of the five points above. Write sentences about it in your notebook.

✏️💻 Technology Extra
Use a camera to take photos of other students doing their presentations. Your teacher will hang the photos in the classroom.

Making a Plan for Your Money

Making a Budget

Work/School
1

Community
2

Home
3

◆ **Vocabulary** Budgets and banking

◆ **Language** *Will, have to,* and *must* • *Wh-* questions and answers

◆ **Pronunciation** Sounds of *ch* and *sh* • Syllable stress

◆ **Culture** Living with parents in the US

Mom, Dad, I want to get an apartment.

How much will it cost?

How do you save money?

Joseph Delva wants to move out of the family home, but he has to save money.

Think and Talk

1. Who are the people in the photo? Where are they?
2. What does Joseph want to do?
3. What does Joseph have to do?
4. What is your plan for saving money?

Gather Your Thoughts

What are your plans for spending your money? Make an idea map in your notebook. Here is an example.

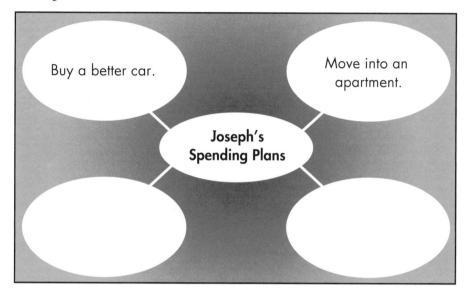

Buy a better car.

Move into an apartment.

Joseph's Spending Plans

What's the Problem?

If you want to save money, you have to make a plan. Why is it difficult to make a money plan, or a budget? Think about this or talk with a partner.

Setting Goals

Think about your answer to the question in What's the Problem? What can you do to save money? Check ✔ your goals.

❑ **1.** Learn about saving money.
❑ **2.** Know my income.
❑ **3.** Know my expenses.
❑ **4.** Set saving goals.
❑ **5.** Make a budget.
❑ **6.** Get another job.
❑ **7.** Another goal: _____

Vocabulary

Listen and repeat. Circle new words. Get meanings from a classmate, your teacher, or a dictionary. Write the words and their meanings.

budget

goal

plan

Opposites

expenses   income

spend   save

_____
your word

_____
your word

Making a Plan

◆ Look at income and expenses

◆ Use *will, have to,* and *must*

deposit

What is in a budget?

◆ **Reading Tip**   A chart can help you understand what you read. Read the paragraph below the chart as your teacher reads it aloud. Then study the chart. How does the reading help you understand the chart?

Idiom Watch!
add up
down payment
keep track of

Budget	
Income:	$2,093/month
– Expenses:	
= Savings:	
Savings Goals	
New Car:	$2,000 down payment
Apartment:	$1,600 deposit & first month's rent

Here's your paycheck, Joseph.

A Budget Can Help Dreams Come True!

Making a budget, a plan for your money, is important. A budget will help you save your money. Making a budget can be difficult. You have to include your income, your expenses, and your savings goals. The first part is easy. You add up your income. This is how much money you earn each month. The next part is hard.

How much money do you spend each month? Keep track of all your expenses. Add them up. Then subtract them from your income. The money remaining is what you can save. Save a little money every month. Soon you will have the money you need to reach your goals.

Talk or Write

1. Joseph is making a budget. What are his savings goals?
2. Joseph thinks he can save $200 a month. How long will it take him to save money for a down payment on a car?
3. Why do you think it is hard to know your expenses?

Picture Dictionary   Listen and repeat. Circle new words.

Get meanings from a classmate, your teacher, or a dictionary.
Write the words and their meanings.

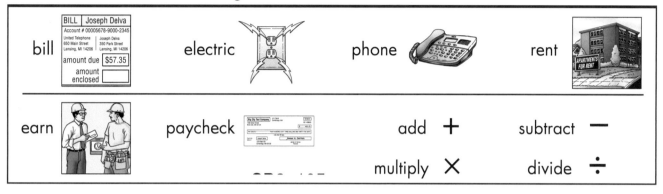

bill	electric	phone	rent

earn	paycheck	add $+$	subtract $-$
		multiply $\times$	divide $\div$

Partner Chat   Interview your partner. Ask about five or
more bills. Write the answers on a chart. Compare your
bills. Put a star next to the answers that are the same.

What bills do you have to pay every month?

I must pay my electric bill.

Me	My Partner
electric	credit card
rent ☆	rent ☆

Grammar Talk: *Will, Have To,* and *Must*

I get a paycheck every Friday.	I **will** get a paycheck next Friday.
He earns a lot of money.	He **has to** work many hours.
The Delvas pay rent for their home.	They **have to** pay rent every month.
Joseph pays for a new shirt.	Joseph **must** pay his credit card bill.

Will, have to, *and* must *go before the verb. Always use the dictionary
form, or base form, of that verb with* will, have to, *and* must. *How does*
have to *change with different subjects?*

Pronunciation Target • Sounds of *ch* and *sh*

🎧 *Listen to your teacher or the audio. Do you hear the difference
between the* ch *sound and the* sh *sound?*

chart, much   shirt, wash

With a partner, practice saying these words.

Activity A   **Partner Chat Follow-Up** Look at your Partner Chat chart.
In your notebook, make new sentences with *will, have to,* and *must.*

<u>Me</u>	<u>My Partner</u>	<u>We Both</u>
I must pay my electric bill.	You have to pay a credit card bill.	We will pay rent.

Activity B   Some of your expenses are the same every month. Some
of your expenses change from month to month. Look back at your
Partner Chat list. List your bills in a chart like this one. Which type of
expenses can you control, the expenses that stay the same or the
expenses that change?

Expenses that Stay the Same		Expenses that Change	
Rent	$600.00	Telephone	$120.00
Car Insurance	$40.00	Food	$210.00

Activity C   Another part of your budget is your income. Your income
is the money that is paid to you. It includes your paycheck and other
money that you earn. Look at Joseph Delva's income. He has two jobs.
What is his income?

Joseph's Income	Paychecks per Month	Multiply	Monthly Income
Big City Taxi—$463.35	4	463.35 x 4	
Lawn Service—$120.00	2	120.00 x 2	
		Total Monthly Income:	

Technology Extra
Check your answers with a calculator.

TASK 1 Track Your Spending
For one week, keep track of all the money that you spend and
where you spend it. You may be surprised to see where it goes!

One Step Up
There is an old saying in
English, "Watch your pennies
and the dollars will take care of
themselves." What does this
mean to you? Do you know a
saying about money in your
language? Tell it to the class.

Saving More Money

◆ Learn about checking and savings accounts

◆ Ask and answer *Wh-* questions (Review)

How do you open a bank account?

flyer
photo ID
for deposit only

◆ Listening Tip 🎧 Look at the photo. Try to guess. Who is talking? What are they talking about? Listen to the conversation. Were you right? Answer the questions with a partner. You can read the words of the conversation on page 118.

Joseph must learn about bank accounts. He will need a checking account to pay bills. He wants to open a savings account also. He needs to save for a deposit on an apartment. He knows that he will have other expenses too.

Talk or Write

1. Who is talking?
2. What does Joseph have to do to open an account?
3. How much does Joseph put into his savings account?
4. Why does the clerk tell Joseph not to endorse his check before he is in the bank?

Partner Chat
Work with a partner. Take turns asking each question below. Write the answers. Compare your answers with your partner.

What is your savings goal?

To buy a better car.

What is your savings goal?

To buy a better car and get a bigger apartment.

What is your bank?

First Bank

When do you pay bills—every week, twice a month, or monthly?

monthly

Who helps make your budget?

my wife

How often do you get a paycheck—every week, twice a month, or monthly?

every week

Vocabulary

Listen and repeat. Circle new words. Get meanings from a classmate, your teacher, or a dictionary. Write the words and their meanings.

Bank Accounts:

checking account

savings account

balance

deposit

endorse

minimum

signature

statement

_____
your word

Grammar Talk: *Wh-* Questions and Answers

What will you do?	I'll go to the bank.
Where is the bank?	It's close to my house.
When will you balance your checkbook?	When I get my bank statement.
Why won't you move now?	Because I have to save money.
Who will help you save?	My parents will help me.
How will they help you?	They will help me make a budget.

The question words above ask for specific information. You cannot answer just yes *or* no.

Activity A Partner Chat Follow-Up Rewrite your savings goals here.

1. Savings Goal: _____

How much will you need? $:_____

2. Savings Goal: _____

How much will you need? $:_____

Activity B Joseph knows that it is important to save monthly. He will put 10% of every paycheck into his savings account. How much will Joseph save every month?

per = for each

Joseph's Income	10% of total (move decimal point to the left)	Multiply by number of paychecks per month
Big City Taxi—$463.35	$46.33	x 4 =
Lawn Service—$120.00		x 2 =
	Total Monthly Savings:	

TASK 2 Make a Savings Plan

A good goal is to save 10% of your income every month. Some weeks you may save less, but try to save every month. It really adds up. Create your savings plan.

1. Add up your total household income.

2. Figure out 10%. This is how much to save each month.

Your Income	10% of total (move decimal point one number to the left)	Multiply by number of paychecks per month
$		
$		
$		
$		
	Total Monthly Savings:	

 **Technology Extra**

Use a calculator.

Spending Less, Saving More

◆ Talk about saving money

◆ Learn about family life in the US

How do you spend your income?

thrift shop
garage sale

◆ Reading Tip   Before you read something, think about the topic. Ask yourself, "What do I already know?" When you do this, you can remember many words that can help you understand what you read. Before you read Mrs. Delva's advice, think about what you already know about saving money. Brainstorm a list of saving tips with your class. Your teacher will write the tips on the board. Then read the advice that Joseph's mother gave him.

Mrs. Delva's Savings Advice

- When you find something you want, wait two weeks before buying. Sometimes you don't want it anymore.
- Make a list before you go shopping. Don't buy things that aren't on your list.
- Buy things on sale.
- Buy things at thrift shops and garage sales.
- Look many places for the same item. Compare prices.
- Rent an apartment with a friend. Share expenses.
- Buy a used car that doesn't use too much gas.
- Don't carry a lot of cash. You will spend it!
- Don't buy food out. Make your food at home.
- When you go out to eat, drink water.

I must be very careful with my money.

Talk or Write

1. What tips will save Joseph the most money? Write them in your notebook.
2. Did the class think of other tips?

What's Your Opinion? Some people say that you should save at least three months' expenses for an emergency. This is called an *emergency fund*. What do you think about this advice?

In the US   Moving Out

In the United States, young people often move out of their family homes after high school. They get their own apartment or share one with friends. They want to live on their own. Often parents want their children to move out. This is part of becoming an adult in the US.

☛ Compare Cultures

Do young people live alone in your home country, or do they live with their parents? Talk with a partner. Then share your ideas with the class.

Pronunciation Target • Syllable Stress

🎧 *Listen to your teacher or the audio say the long words in the vocabulary list. The words have more than one syllable. One of the syllables is stressed. A stressed syllable sounds longer and sometimes louder than unstressed syllables.*

Vocabulary

Listen and repeat. Circle new words. Get meanings from a classmate, your teacher, or a dictionary. Write the words and their meanings.

advice

apartment

cash

cost

emergency

compare

share

---
your word

Idiom Watch!

on your own

Activity A   Is it good for young adults to live with their parents? What is good (+)? What is bad (–)? Make a chart like the one below. Show your chart to your partner. Are your ideas the same or different? Explain.

| Living with Parents | | Living on Your Own | |
(+)	(–)	(+)	(–)
no rent	too many fights	can do what I like	have to cook

Activity B Work with a partner. Look at Joseph's budget. What advice can you give him? How can he save more money? How long will it take Joseph to save $1200.00 if he saves $60.00 a month?

Monthly Income			Savings Goals		
Big City Taxi		$1853.40	1. Deposit on		
Yard Service		$240.00	Apartment		$1200.00
	Total	$2093.40	2. Emergency Fund		0
				Total	$1200.00
Expenses that Stay the Same			**Expenses that Change**		
Rent		$600.00	Food		$200.00
Electric		$120.00	Clothing		$100.00
Car Insurance		$300.00	Telephone		$200.00
Renters Insurance		$50.00	Entertainment		$100.00
	Total A	$1070.00		Total B	$600.00
Total A + Total B = Total Expenses = $1670.00					

Activity C Work with a partner. Read Joseph's budget as a pie chart. How much does Joseph spend monthly? How much does Joseph save?

> misc. = miscellaneous

10% misc. expenses

10% savings

80% expenses

TASK 3 Where Did the Money Go?
Look back at the spending journal you did for Task 1. Write the information you gathered in a chart like this one.

Expenses that Stay the Same	Expenses that Change	
	fast food	$25.00
	greeting card	$2.50

Make Your Budget

Create a monthly budget. Look at it with your family.

Get Ready

1. Get a chart from your teacher.
2. Write your savings goals from page 53.
3. Write your income from Task 2, page 53.
4. Write your expenses from Task 3, page 56.

Do the Work

Monthly Income		Savings Goals	
1. 2.	Total	1. 2. 3. Emergency Fund	Total
Expenses that Stay the Same		**Expenses that Change**	
Rent Electric Car Insurance Renters Insurance	Total A	Food Clothing Telephone Entertainment	Total B
Total A + Total B = Total Expenses =			

Present Your Project

Show your budget to everyone who lives with you. Everyone must understand the budget. You have to work as a team to reach savings goals. Does anyone see how to save more money? What changes will you make to the plan? Remember, goals can change. If your savings goals change, you have to change the budget.

Writing Extension   In your notebook, write about making a budget. What was difficult? How do you feel now that you have a plan?

Bargain Shopping

Getting a Good Deal

Home
1

Work/School
2

Community
3

◆ **Vocabulary** Shopping • Places to shop • Clothing and electronics

◆ **Language** Comparative adjectives • Compound sentences with *and . . . too* and with *or*

◆ **Pronunciation** Sounds of *th* • Sounds of *s* and *st*

◆ **Culture** Shopping in the US

Can you find bargains?

Ann Judson takes her children shopping for things for school.

Think and Talk

1. Where are the Judsons going?
2. What will they do?
3. How do you think Ann feels?
4. How can they find bargains?

What's Your Opinion? What's good or bad about shopping?

Picture Dictionary   Listen and repeat. Circle new words.
Get meanings from a classmate, your teacher, or a dictionary.
Write the words and their meanings.

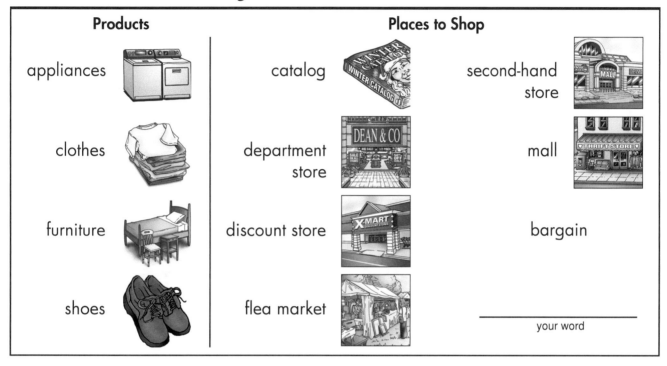

Products	Places to Shop	
appliances	catalog	second-hand store
clothes	department store	mall
furniture	discount store	bargain
shoes	flea market	_____ your word

Gather Your Thoughts   What products do you buy? Where can
you shop? Make an idea map in your notebook. Here's an example.
Use the words in the Picture Dictionary and other words you know.

What's The Problem?   What makes shopping difficult? Think
about it, or talk with a partner.

Setting Goals   Think about some things your family needs. How
can you get bargains? Check ✔ all that apply.

❑ 1. Compare prices.
❑ 2. Compare clothing.
❑ 3. Shop for bargains.

❑ 4. Consider second-hand shopping.
❑ 5. Learn new ways to shop.
❑ 6. Another goal: _____

Looking for School Clothes

◆ Identify clothing and prices

◆ Use comparative adjectives

Where can you look for information to find bargains?

◆ Reading Tip   Pictures can help you understand the information you read. Look at the pictures to find items you need. Use the pictures to help you understand the words. Use the pictures and words in these ads to learn about the sales.

| briefs |
| cotton |
| denim |
| item |
| leather |
| pocket |
| ads = advertisements |

Ann helps her twins plan for school shopping.

Talk or Write

1. What clothing do you see?
2. How much can you save if you buy two pairs of sandals?
3. What are the T-shirt sizes?
4. Which articles of clothing are for men?

Picture Dictionary   Listen and repeat. Circle new words.
Get meanings from a classmate, your teacher, or a dictionary.
Write the words and their meanings.

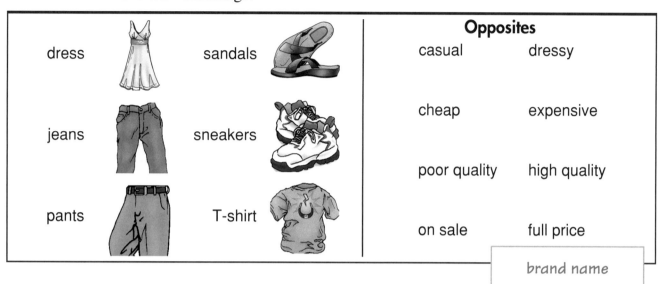

dress		sandals	
jeans		sneakers	
pants		T-shirt	

Opposites

casual	dressy
cheap	expensive
poor quality	high quality
on sale	full price

brand name

Class Chat   Walk around. Ask questions. Write answers
in your notebook.

Name	Clothing Item	Where did you buy it?
Fayed	dress	department store

Nice dress! Where did you buy it?

Thanks. At a department store.

Grammar Talk: Comparative Adjectives

The sneakers are **cheaper** at the discount store.

I like **more casual** clothes.

Brand name jeans are **more expensive** in the mall than in a discount store.

You will get a **better** bargain in a second-hand store.

There are three different ways of making comparisons. What are they?
What word do you use to compare one thing to another?

Pronunciation Target • Sounds of *th*
🎧 *Listen to your teacher or the audio. Do you hear the difference between the two sounds of* th?

thing, both   father, that

Activity A **Class Chat Follow-Up** Look at your Class Chat notes. In your notebook, write sentences about your classmates' clothes.

Fayed bought her dress at a department store.

Activity B Talk to five different people. Ask them where they like to shop and why. Take notes in your notebook.

I shop at a discount shoe store because it is cheaper.

It's better to go to the mall. The shoes are nicer.

Write sentences. Share with the class.

Miriam likes to shop at the mall because she finds better quality clothes.

Activity C Work in a group. Look at newspaper and magazine ads for clothes. Make a chart like the one below. Write three items you want to buy, a place where you can buy each, and the prices.

Item	Shopping Place	Price
dress	department store	$59.99

TASK 1 Compare As You Shop

Choose one item you need to buy. Find the same item in different newspaper ads, magazine ads, and store catalogs. Compare the items. Use the chart.

One Step Up
With a partner, talk about your shopping choice. Which one will you buy? Why?

	Price	Description	Quality
Newspaper			
Magazine			
Catalog			

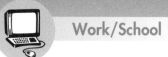
A Shopping Spree

◆ Identify clothing

◆ Compare shopping issues in different cultures

Do you find out about bargains on television?

◆ Listening Tip 🎧 Close your eyes and pretend you are listening to a commercial. Write the items that are advertised. Listen again. You can read the words on page 119.

Ann works at Better Bargains Superstore. They are having a big sale. She is helping customers.

Talk or Write

1. Where are the bargains?
2. What items are advertised?
3. Listen for the comparative adjectives in the TV ad. Write them in your notebook. Write three sentences using the adjectives.

Picture Dictionary Listen and repeat. Circle new words.
Get meanings from a classmate, your teacher, or a dictionary.
Write the words and their meanings.

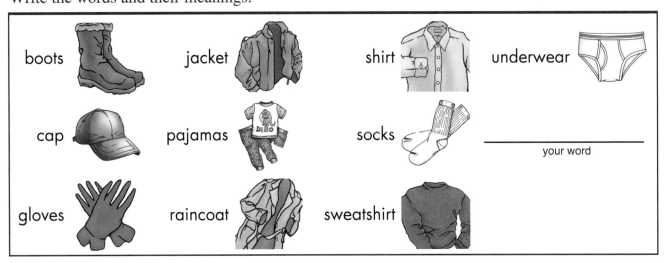

boots

jacket

shirt

underwear

cap

pajamas

socks

_____
your word

gloves

raincoat

sweatshirt

In the US Learn How to Shop

currency

interest

It is fun to shop in the US, but remember these things:

- In most stores, customers don't bargain for lower prices, but they look for discounts.
- In almost all states, customers have to pay sales tax.
- You can buy products on credit with a credit card. Credit cards charge interest on the money that you owe.
- You may not understand the sizes for clothes and shoes in the US. Try clothes on before you buy them.

☞ **Compare Cultures**

Talk to five classmates. Ask these questions:

• In your home country, where do you shop for clothes?

• Do you bargain to get lower prices?

• Do you know the value of the US dollar in your currency?

• What system of clothes and shoe sizes do you use?

Record the answers in your notebook. Share with the class.

Name	Country	Shopping Place	OK to Bargain?	$ Value	Size

Activity A

Work with a partner. Convert the metric sizes below to the US system.

> Divide the centimeters by 2.5 to get inches.

	Mr. Lafitte		**Mrs. Lafitte**	
	Metric	US	Metric	US
Height	175 cm	70 in.	155 cm	_____
Waist	102 cm	_____	85 cm	_____
Pants Length	85 cm	_____	75 cm	_____

Activity B

Work with your partner. Write a list of clothing items Mr. and Mrs. Lafitte can buy. Write a price for each item. This state charges 6% tax. What is the total that the Lafittes will have to pay?

> To calculate the tax, you multiply the total times 0.06.

Item	**Price**	**6% Tax**	**Subtotal**
jacket	$79.99	$4.80	$84.79
_____	_____	_____	_____
_____	_____	_____	_____
_____	_____	_____	_____
		Total	_____

TASK 2 List Clothing Sizes

Work in groups. Do you buy clothes for another person? Complete a chart like this one.

Person's Name:		Relationship:
	US Size	Home Country Size
dress		
jacket		
pants		
shirt		
shoes		
other:		

Community

Surfing the Internet

◆ Talk about shopping on the Internet

◆ Use compound sentences with *and . . . too* and with *or*

Do you shop on the Internet?

❑ Often ❑ Sometimes ❑ Never

Idiom Watch!
surfing the Internet

◆ Reading Tip   An Internet shopping page lists many products. Scan the list below. Which words do you know? Circle the words you don't know. Can you guess their meanings? How many words for electronic products sound or look the same in your first language? Write the words in English and in your first language.

Go To: http://

Electronics

Super Low Prices!

$1,299.99
Notebook Computer

$169.99
DVD Player with Built-in VCR

$279.99
Digital Camera

$119.99
20-inch TV

▶ More Notebook Computers
▶ More DVD Players
▶ More Digital Cameras
▶ More Televisions

Talk or Write

1. What can you find on this page?
2. What other items can you shop for? Name three.
3. Do you ever use the Internet to shop?

Picture Dictionary Listen and repeat. Circle new words.
Get meanings from a classmate, your teacher, or a dictionary.
Write the words and their meanings.

accessories    camcorder   electronic game   wireless phone

audio   camera   fax

wireless phone = cellular phone   electronics

_____
your word

Class Chat Walk around. Ask questions. Write answers.

What can you buy on the Internet?

Cameras and games.

Name	What can you buy on the Internet?
Claudia	Cameras and games.

Grammar Talk: Compound Sentences with *And . . . Too* and with *Or*

We shop in stores, **and** we can shop on the Internet **too.**

Do you want to buy clothes, **or** do you want to go to lunch?

What form do you use to say two different things? What form do you use to decide on doing one of two different things?

Pronunciation Target • Sounds of *s* and *st*

 Listen to your teacher or the audio.

sale	store
see	standard
socks	stop

Practice with a partner saying these words. Find other words that begin with s. *Make a two-column chart in your notebook. Say and write the* s *and* st *words.*

Activity A Talk with a partner. You have $80. Look at a shopping site on the Internet, or look at store catalogs and newspaper flyers.

- Find two things that you can buy. Write a sentence about them with *and*.
- Find two things that you like, but you can only afford to buy one of them. Write a sentence about them with *or*.

I can buy a pair of sneakers, and I can buy a pair of jeans too.

I can buy a CD player, or I can buy a computer game.

Activity B Work in a small group. Talk about the advantages and disadvantages of shopping on the Internet. Write compound sentences about shopping on the Internet, in stores, or through catalogs.

advantage	+
disadvantage	−

Shopping on the Internet

Advantages (+)	Disadvantages (−)
bigger market	credit card fraud
stay home	shipping charges
more choices	cannot see merchandise

On the Internet, I have more choices, and I can stay home too.

In the stores, I can pay with cash, or I can use a credit card.

 TASK 3 Compare Ads

Select an item you want to buy. Compare three ads: a newspaper ad, a catalog ad, and an Internet ad. Complete the chart.

	Newspaper	Catalog	Internet
Place to buy			
Description			
Cost			
Tax			
Shipping and handling			
Total			

Find a Bargain

Read ads, compare items, and find a bargain.

Get Ready

In a group, select an item that you need to buy:

- clothes for teenagers
- a computer
- a toy for small children
- a car
- furniture
- an appliance

Each person brings an ad from a different place. Look for special offers, coupons, or delivery charges. Compare the ads, and select one item.

Do the Work

Get an idea map from your teacher. Write information in it about the product. Create a poster with the following information:

- product selected
- brand
- shopping place
- size or color
- price
- total cost (including tax and shipping charge)
- reasons for selecting the product

Present Your Project

Select one person in the group to report to the class.

Writing Extension Write about the item that your group selected. Explain why you chose that item.

Technology Extra

Go to the Internet. Find three shopping links. List one product you find to buy in each of them. Calculate the total cost.

Equal Rights

Protecting Your Legal Rights

Work/School
1

Home
2

Community
3

◆ **Vocabulary** Rights in the workplace • Equality and discrimination

◆ **Language** Modals: *may, should, could, would* • Present continuous (review) and past continuous

◆ **Pronunciation** Sounds of *a* • Reductions

◆ **Culture** Equal rights and the law in the US

machine repairperson

Do you ever feel discriminated against?

Amara is looking for a job as a machine repairperson. No one will hire her. Her aunt and uncle think she should look for an easier job. She feels discriminated against.

Think and Talk

1. What is Amara doing?

2. What is she looking for?

3. Do you think she will find the job she wants?

Gather Your Thoughts
What jobs do you really want? Are they traditional jobs for a person like you? In your notebook, make an idea map like this one.

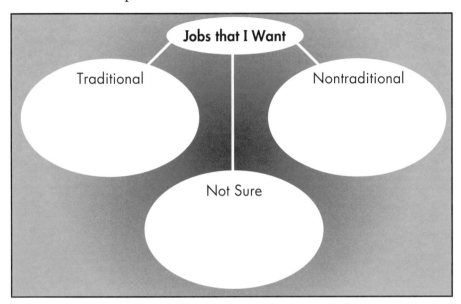

Jobs that I Want

Traditional

Nontraditional

Not Sure

What's the Problem?
Do you have a problem getting the job you want? What are your challenges? Think about these questions, or talk with a partner.

Setting Goals
Think about your answers to the questions above. What can you do about the problem? Check ✔ your goals.

❑ **1.** Identify my skills.
❑ **2.** Prepare for challenges in a job interview.
❑ **3.** Learn about my rights.
❑ **4.** Protect myself against discrimination.
❑ **5.** Another goal: _____

Vocabulary

Listen and repeat. Circle new words. Get meanings from a classmate, your teacher, or a dictionary. Write the words and their meanings.

discriminate

discrimination

equal

hire

rights

nontraditional

traditional

challenge

age

ethnicity

gender

_____
your word

Getting the Job You Want

◆ Talk about qualifications and challenges
◆ Use the modals *may, should, could, would*

Did you ever have trouble getting the job you wanted?

◆ Listening Tip 🎧 A picture can give you some information about the topic. Look at the photo and then listen to the job interview. You can read the words on page 119. Listen again and try to follow along with the conversation.

machine repair
operator
position
recommendation
textile plant

Ben Sanders interviews Amara.

Talk or Write

1. Where is Amara?
2. What job is she applying for?
3. What job does the interviewer think she should apply for?
4. Do you think she'll get the job she wants?

Class Chat   Walk around. Ask questions. Write answers in your chart.

Did you ever apply for a job you didn't get?

Yes, I did. I applied for a job as a truck driver.

Why didn't you get it?

They thought I was too old.

Your Name	Job You Applied for	Why didn't you get it?
Rafael	truck driver	too old

Vocabulary

Listen and repeat. Circle new words. Get meanings from a classmate, your teacher, or a dictionary. Write the words and their meanings.

attitude

background

experience

opportunity

license

prejudice

qualifications

resume

Grammar Talk: Modals: *May, Should, Could, Would*

Amara **may** get a job.	She **may not** get the job she wants.
She **could** repair the machines.	Many people **couldn't** do that.
Maybe she **should** start in an easier job.	She **shouldn't** have to take another job.
I **would** find out about my rights.	I **would not** accept the interviewer's answer.

Can you tell how may, could, should *and* would *are different from other verbs? They do not have an s in the third person singular. They are followed by the base form of a verb.*

Pronunciation Target • Sounds of *a*

 Listen to your teacher or the audio. Do you hear two different sounds of the vowel a?

and	sales
factory	may
ads	age

With a partner, practice saying these words. Write other words in two columns in your notebook.

Activity A   With a partner, role-play the conversation between Amara and the interviewer. You can read the words on page 119. Practice saying the words with *a*. Add your own sentences to the conversation. What would you say?

Activity B   Work with a group. Read the thank-you note Amara sent to Ben Sanders. Write answers to the questions.

August 4, 2004

Dear Mr. Sanders:

I would like to thank you for interviewing me for the position of machine repairperson. I am very interested in that position. I have two years of experience working with the same kind of equipment you use in your factory. I could be good for your company. Please contact me if you should require more information.

I hope that you may consider my application favorably.

Sincerely,
Amara Mirembe
Amara Mirembe

1. How does Amara begin and end the letter?
2. In which order does she do the following? Number the items.

    _____ a. mention her previous work as a machine repairperson

    _____ b. thank Mr. Sanders for seeing her

    _____ c. offer to give him more information

    _____ d. hope to get the job

3. What would you change in the letter?

 TASK 1 Write a Thank-You Letter

Choose a job you would like to apply for. Answer the questions.

Job: _____

1. Why did you choose this job?
2. What are your qualifications?
3. What are the challenges in getting this job?

Now write a thank-you note in your notebook. Follow Amara's model.

It's Everyone's World

◆ Learn about legal rights in the US

◆ Prepare for job interviews

Where does discrimination happen?

◆ Reading Tip   Read the title. Talk to a partner about what you might find in this pamphlet. Read the pamphlet twice. Then tell your partner in your own words what it means.

> access
> encourage
> expectation
> success

EQUAL EXPECTATIONS FOR EQUAL SUCCESS

The world of work in the 21st century offers many opportunities to men and women. In the past, families expected boys to succeed. Parents and teachers encouraged them at home and in school. Women worked mostly as teachers or nurses. Today, US laws provide for equal access to all jobs. People want equal pay for equal work. Teachers and parents should have high expectations for both girls and boys.

Local and national organizations help women and girls to get information about higher paying jobs and training programs. They also provide information about strategies for interviews, legal rights, and nontraditional jobs. For more information, contact your local job center.

Amara, maybe you should apply for an easier job.

You could learn more about your rights.

Talk or Write

1. How is work in the 21st century different from the past?
2. What can parents and teachers do to help boys and girls have equal success?
3. Where can women get information about higher paying jobs?
4. What can Amara do?

In the US   Laws against Discrimination

The following are federal laws against job discrimination:

- **Title VII of the Civil Rights Act of 1964** forbids job discrimination based on race, color, religion, gender, or national origin.

- **The Equal Pay Act of 1963 (EPA)** says that men and women who do equal work at the same work site must be paid an equal wage.

- The **Age Discrimination in Employment Act of 1967 (ADEA)** protects people who are 40 years of age or older against job discrimination based on age.

- **Title I of the Americans with Disabilities Act of 1990 (ADA)** forbids employment discrimination against qualified people with disabilities.

- The **Civil Rights Act of 1991** provides for compensation in cases of job discrimination.

The **Equal Employment Opportunity Commission (EEOC)** protects us against job discrimination.

☛ Compare Cultures

How do the laws of your home country protect you against discrimination?

- Write sentences about the laws in your home country and in the US.
- Talk with a partner.

Vocabulary

Listen and repeat. Circle new words. Get meanings from a classmate, your teacher, or a dictionary. Write the words and their meanings.

compensation

disability

employment

forbid

law

legal

protect

provide

wage

_____
your word

_____
your word

Activity A   Work in a small group. Talk about ways that you or someone in your family could be discriminated against. Write examples in a chart like this one.

Who?	Why?	Where could they have a problem?
My sister	disability	no access to bathroom in restaurant

Activity B   Talk with a partner. Do you treat boys and girls in different ways? Is there anything you should change about your attitude? In your notebook write things you should do and things you could do.

I should ask my son to do housework.

One Step Up
Talk with a partner. Tell one thing that is different about raising children in your country.

Activity C   Some questions are not legal in a job interview. Here are two examples:

- How many children do you have?
- Are you pregnant?

pregnant = going to have a baby

You may tell the interviewer, "That question doesn't relate to the good work I can do for your company." In a group, talk about questions like this and ways to answer them.

 TASK 2   Prepare for a Job Interview
You have an interview for the job you selected for Task 1. Remember the challenges. Write three things you can do to prepare for the challenges. In your notebook, write three questions you may be asked and the answers you should give.

Name: _____   Job:_____

Challenge(s): _____

What to do: **1.** _____

2. _____

3. _____

Fighting Discrimination

◆ Learn how to deal with discrimination

◆ Use present continuous (review) and past continuous

> applicant
> diverse
> follow-up letter

What groups in your community have talents that aren't being used?

◆ Reading Tip   When you read, it helps to predict what will happen next. Read this conversation between Ben and his boss. What do you think Ben will do next?

Talk or Write
1. Who is talking to Ben Sanders?
2. What is Ben doing?
3. Why does Ben's boss want to call in Amara for a second interview?
4. What do you think will happen next?

What's Your Opinion?   Should companies have to hire people from diverse groups in their community?

Class Chat   Walk around. Ask questions. Write the answers in your chart.

What do you need help with?

My landlord is discriminating against me. I want to learn about my legal rights.

What could you do?

I could go to a legal agency.

Name	What do you need help with?	What could you do?
Hans	my rights as a tenant	find a legal agency

Vocabulary

Listen and repeat. Circle new words. Get meanings from a classmate, your teacher, or a dictionary. Write the words and their meanings.

- agency
- applicant
- apply
- follow-up
- landlord
- tenant

Grammar Talk: Present Continuous and Past Continuous

Present Continuous	**Past Continuous**
Amara's uncle **is giving** her advice.	Her aunt and uncle **were trying** to help.
Are you **learning** about your rights?	Yes, I **was reading** an article about equal rights.
Is Amara **trying** to find a solution?	She **wasn't taking** the operator's job.

What is the difference between the present continuous and past continuous?

Pronunciation Target • Reductions

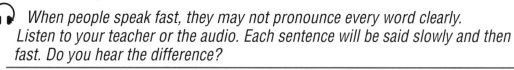

🎧   *When people speak fast, they may not pronounce every word clearly. Listen to your teacher or the audio. Each sentence will be said slowly and then fast. Do you hear the difference?*

Would you like coffee or tea?

We were learning about our rights.

Could you start working next Monday?

We are cooking beans and bacon.

Amara is going to fight back.

I don't know.

Activity A   **Class Chat Follow-Up**   Look at your Class Chat chart.
In your notebook write sentences about your classmates' problems and
what they can do.

Hans is going to a legal agency to learn about his rights as a tenant.

Activity B   Talk to a partner. Ask what your partner was doing before
coming to the United States.

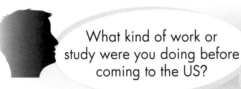

What kind of work or
study were you doing before
coming to the US?

I was working
with computers, and I was
studying English too.

Work with your partner. Write a paragraph about what you <u>were doing</u>
before coming to the US.

Exchange papers. Check your partner's English. Try to guess things
about your partner. Write what your partner <u>wasn't doing</u> before coming
to the US. Then write some things your partner <u>isn't doing now.</u>

Exchange papers with your partner. Check your partner's sentences
about you. Are they true or false? Make the false sentences true.

TASK 3   Discuss Discrimination
Work with a partner. Read the stories. After you read each story, stop
and talk about how to fight against this type of discrimination.

physical disability
principal

Story 1	Story 2	Story 3
A Korean family goes to a nice restaurant. The father asks for a table by the window, but the manager seats the family in the back of the restaurant. An American family comes in and asks for a table by the window. The manager seats them near the window.	The principal of a school fires an older woman teacher. He tells her that the school is paying her too much money. He says that the school will hire a younger teacher for less money.	A man applies for a job as a computer programmer. He has the training, experience, and good recommendations. He writes in his application that he has a physical disability. He doesn't get an interview.

Make a Complaint

Complete a discrimination complaint form.

Get Ready

Think of a case of discrimination that you know about. You may use Amara Mirembe's story or one of the stories in Task 3.

Do the Work

Complete the complaint form. Your teacher will give you a copy.

DISCRIMINATION COMPLAINT FORM

1. Name: _____ Address: _____

   Phone (home): _____ (work): _____

2. Basis of the discrimination

   ☐ race ☐ color ☐ religion ☐ national origin ☐ retaliation

   ☐ age ☐ gender ☐ disability ☐ marital status ☐ sexual orientation

   ☐ other (specify): _____

3. Dates of the discrimination: from _____ to _____

4. Name of person(s) who you believe discriminated against you

   Name: _____ Job title: _____

   Name: _____ Job title: _____

5. Because of this discrimination I was

   ☐ fired ☐ not hired ☐ not promoted ☐ not given benefits ☐ paid less

   ☐ other: _____

6. Details of complaint _____

   _____

   _____

   Signature _____ Date _____

Present Your Project

Tell the class about the discrimination and your complaint. Read the form you completed.

✏️ **Writing Extension**   Write a short cover letter to send with the complaint form.

✂️🖥️ **Technology Extra**

Find the Internet address for the Equal Employment Opportunity Commission of the US government. Go there and find a page that interests you. Share it with the class.

Paying Taxes

Understanding Paychecks and Taxes

Work/School
1

Home
2

Community
3

◆ **Vocabulary** Paychecks • Taxes

◆ **Language** Verbs followed by infinitives • Order of adjectives

◆ **Pronunciation** Sounds of *e* • Sounds of *t* and *d*

◆ **Culture** Taxation in the US

celebrate
confused
missing

Do you know what to expect when you are paid?

Puri gets his first paycheck in the US. He wants to celebrate, but some of his money is missing. He is confused.

Think and Talk

1. What is Puri thinking?
2. Who can help him?
3. Did you ever feel like this?

What's Your Opinion? What should Puri say to his employer?

Picture Dictionary   Listen and repeat. Circle new words.

Get meanings from a classmate, your teacher, or a dictionary.
Write the words and their meanings.

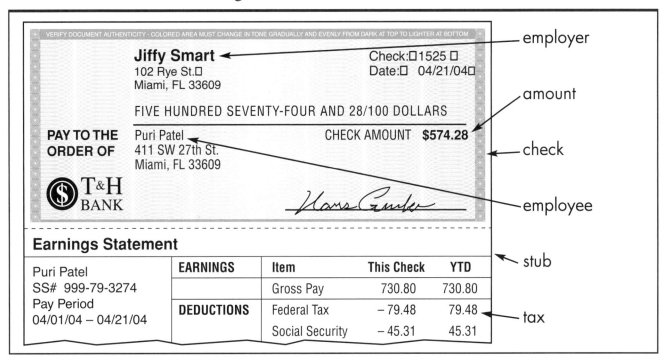

Jiffy Smart — employer
102 Rye St.
Miami, FL 33609
Check: 1525
Date: 04/21/04

FIVE HUNDRED SEVENTY-FOUR AND 28/100 DOLLARS — amount

PAY TO THE ORDER OF   Puri Patel
411 SW 27th St.
Miami, FL 33609

CHECK AMOUNT **$574.28**

— check

T&H BANK — employee

— stub

Earnings Statement

	EARNINGS	Item	This Check	YTD
Puri Patel SS# 999-79-3274		Gross Pay	730.80	730.80
Pay Period 04/01/04 – 04/21/04	DEDUCTIONS	Federal Tax	– 79.48	79.48
		Social Security	– 45.31	45.31

— tax

Gather Your Thoughts   Even people born in the US find

paychecks and taxes confusing. Where can you get information about
paychecks and taxes? Talk about ideas with your teacher. Make a chart
like this in your notebook. Write the answers on your chart.

Ways to Learn about Taxes and Paychecks

read tax forms

ask friends

What's the Problem?   Why do you have to pay taxes? How can

you learn more about taxes? Think about this, or talk with a partner.

Setting Goals   Think about your answers to the questions above.

What can you do about the problem? Check ✔ your goals.

❑ **1.** Learn to read my paycheck.
❑ **2.** Ask questions about taxes.
❑ **3.** Get information from my employer.

❑ **4.** Learn about tax forms.
❑ **5.** Another goal: _____

Where Does All the Money Go?

◆ Understand your paycheck

◆ Use verbs followed by infinitives

Do you understand your paycheck?

◆ **Reading Tip** If you don't understand what you are reading, try reading again. Read the parts that you don't understand more slowly. Now read this employee handout. What parts are hard to understand?

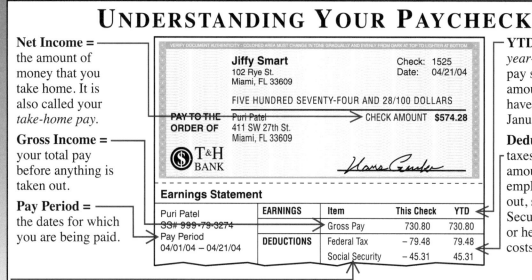

UNDERSTANDING YOUR PAYCHECK

Net Income = the amount of money that you take home. It is also called your *take-home pay.*

Gross Income = your total pay before anything is taken out.

Pay Period = the dates for which you are being paid.

YTD = *year-to-date.* Most pay stubs show the amount that you have earned since January 1.

Deductions = taxes and other amounts that your employer takes out, such as Social Security payments or health insurance costs.

VERIFY DOCUMENT AUTHENTICITY · COLORED AREA MUST CHANGE IN TONE GRADUALLY AND EVENLY FROM DARK AT TOP TO LIGHTER AT BOTTOM

Jiffy Smart
102 Rye St.
Miami, FL 33609

Check: 1525
Date: 04/21/04

FIVE HUNDRED SEVENTY-FOUR AND 28/100 DOLLARS

PAY TO THE ORDER OF Puri Patel
411 SW 27th St.
Miami, FL 33609

CHECK AMOUNT **$574.28**

Ⓢ **T&H BANK**

Earnings Statement

Puri Patel	EARNINGS	Item	This Check	YTD
SS# 999-79-3274		Gross Pay	730.80	730.80
Pay Period 04/01/04 – 04/21/04	DEDUCTIONS	Federal Tax	– 79.48	79.48
		Social Security	– 45.31	45.31

Withholdings = the money that your employer takes out of your paycheck to pay federal and state taxes. This money is sent to the government in your name. If withholdings are not taken out every pay period, you will have to pay a big amount when taxes are due on April 15 of the next year.

Now I know where the money went.

Puri's employer gives him information about his paycheck. Puri learns many new words. Now he can read his paycheck.

Talk or Write

1. Is gross income larger or smaller than net income?
2. What is a pay period?
3. What is another word for net income?

Partner Chat   Think about your first job. What did you want to know? Tell your partner two things you wanted to know. Use the words in the box. Take turns asking questions.

| my pay | more English | my schedule |
| safety rules | my vacation | medical benefits |

What did you want to know?

I wanted to know my pay.

Name	What did you want to know?	What else did you want to know?
Naomi	my pay	my schedule

Vocabulary

Listen and repeat. Circle new words. Get meanings from a classmate, your teacher, or a dictionary. Write the words and their meanings.

- deduction
- gross income
- health insurance
- net income
- withhold
- withholdings

_____
your word

Grammar Talk: Verbs Followed by Infinitives

I know my pay.	I **have to know** my pay.
You learn about taxes.	You **want to learn** about taxes.
Puri speaks to his employer.	Puri **needs to speak** to his employer.
We speak English.	We **want to speak** English.
They work on the house.	They **need to work** on the house.

When you add a helping verb (have, want, or need), *change the original verb to its dictionary form, the base form. Add* to *before the base form. Study the sentences above. Which verb changes? Which stays the same?*

Pronunciation Target • Sounds of e

🎧 *Listen to your teacher or the audio. Do you hear the different sounds of* e? *On the end of a word, the vowel* e *can be silent.*

Short e	**Long e**		**Silent e**
net	he	need	make
check	we	speak	date
get	she	agree	

Activity A **Partner Chat Follow-Up** Look at your Partner Chat chart. In your notebook, write sentences using *have* and *need*.

Naomi has to know her schedule. Naomi needs to know her pay.

Activity B With a partner, find the following items on Puri's paycheck, page 83. Answer the questions.

gross income
− deductions
net income

1. What is Puri's gross income? _____

2. What is the pay period? _____

3. What is Puri's Social Security number? _____

4. What is Puri's take-home pay? _____

5. What is the total of Puri's deductions? _____

Activity C Use the words in the box to fill in the blanks.

| amount | deductions | ✔employer | net income | taxes | withheld |

Puri was very happy. His _____employer_____ gave him his first US paycheck! At
                                         1
first, Puri thought the _____ on the check was too low. Now he knows
                                    2
that some money is _____ from each paycheck. The stub shows his gross
                              3
income and all the _____. His employer withholds money for
                              4
_____ and Social Security. The amount that is left after deductions is
        5
called his _____.
                    6

TASK 1   Read Paychecks

Your teacher will give you copies of paychecks and stubs with personal information covered. In a small group, look at the checks. Can your group find the gross pay, net pay, pay rate, pay period, federal tax, and other deductions? How are the paychecks the same? How are they different? With the class, make a list of all the deductions.

Taxes—How Much Can You Control?

◆ Learn about W-4 forms

◆ Use adjectives in sentences

---

confused
confusing

Do you have to fill out confusing forms?

❏ Often ❏ Sometimes ❏ Never

◆ Reading Tip Before you begin reading, know what you want to learn. After you read Puri's story, you will answer the questions below. Read the questions first. Now read Puri's story for the answers to the questions.

Puri's Story

I am Puri Patel, and I am from India. I came to the United States six months ago. I have a wife, but I do not have children yet. My wife and I live with my uncle and his family. I want a big family. I love children.

I like to go to English classes every day. I learn to speak, read, and write in English. Mostly, I want to speak. If I can't speak, I can't work.

I got a new job three weeks ago. I work at a small store called Jiffy Smart. During the first week, I had to answer questions about my family for taxes. I was confused, but my employer helped me.

Talk or Write

1. How long has Puri been in the United States?
2. Is Puri married or single?
3. Does he have a large family?
4. What classes does Puri take?
5. Where does Puri work?

Partner Chat   Look at the list of questions. Take turns reading the questions aloud with your partner. Are the questions polite or impolite, or are you not sure? Talk about your answers.

Do you like your new job?

Question	Polite	Impolite	Not Sure
Do you like your new job?	X		
Are you happily married?		X	
When are you going to have a baby?			
How much money do you make?			
Are you a natural blonde?			

Vocabulary

Listen and repeat. Circle new words. Get meanings from a classmate, your teacher, or a dictionary. Write the words and their meanings.

married

single

husband

wife

spouse

claim

complete

dependent

support

Grammar Talk: Order of Adjectives

Puri is **happy** about his **new** job.   He works at a **small, busy** store.
Puri wants a **big** family.   He likes a **noisy, happy** home.

Where do adjectives come in the sentence? What do you do when you have more than one adjective?

Pronunciation Target • Sounds of *t* and *d*

🎧 *Listen to your teacher or the audio. Do you hear the difference between* t *and* d?
tax, talk, extra   dinner, dependent, deduction

With a partner, practice saying these words. Place a sheet of paper in front of your lips. You should feel a puff of air when you pronounce t, *and no air when you pronounce* d.

Activity A   Partner Chat Follow-Up With your partner, answer the Partner Chat questions. Write the sentences in your notebook. Underline the adjectives.

Activity B 🎧 When you get a new job, you need to complete a W-4 form. Listen to the audio. Complete the explanation of a W-4 form with the words in the box.

> Internal Revenue Service (IRS)
> W-4

claim	dependents	net	spouse	taxes	withhold

Form W-4 tells how much money to _____ from your paycheck for

1

taxes. You write how many allowances you want to claim. If no one else can

_____ you as a dependent, you enter 1 for yourself. If you are married,

2

you may want to claim your _____ too. You can claim any children you

3

support as _____. When you claim more dependents, you take home

4

more _____ pay. However, you may have to pay more

5

_____ to the IRS in April.

6

Activity C Interview a classmate that you don't know well. Use the answers to write a story. Rewrite the story in your notebook. Share the story with the class.

1. What is your full name?
2. Where are you from?
3. When did you come to the US?

4. Are you married or single?
5. Do you have children?
6. What do you like to do?

_____ 's Story

   This is _____. He/she is from _____. He/she came

to the US _____ (number) (months/years) ago. _____ is (single/married)

and has _____ (number) children. He/she likes to _____.

TASK 2 Fill Out a W-4 Form

Get a copy of a W-4 form from your teacher. Fill it out for yourself or for Puri. You can find information for Puri on his paycheck on page 83 and in his story on page 87.

Getting a Refund

◆ Learn about government tax forms

◆ Understand the reasons for taxes

How do you feel about paying taxes?

◆ Listening Tip 🎧 Taking notes is a good way to remember what you hear. Numbers are difficult to remember. Now listen to Puri's conversation with his wife, Nadya. Write the names of the tax forms. You can read the words on page 119.

accountant
system
1040 form
W-2 form

Idiom Watch!

do your taxes

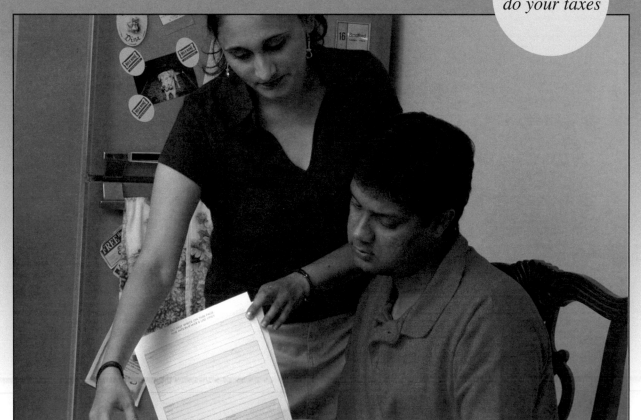

Puri and Nadya are doing their tax forms.

Talk or Write

1. What are Puri and Nadya talking about?
2. Why does she think that he can learn about the tax system?
3. What tax form did Puri get from his job?

In the US Why Do People Pay Taxes?

The Internal Revenue Service (IRS) is the federal agency that collects taxes on income. States may also collect income taxes. Income taxes pay for schools and teachers, libraries and courthouses, roads and parks, police and firefighters, the military, and much more. Some people do not like taxes. They think the government takes too much money. Others want the government to pay for more services such as health care, child care, and welfare programs. This would mean more taxes. There will always be people who disagree on taxes.

Whether you agree with taxes or not, you must remember to fill out a federal income tax form at the end of each year. This form and the money you owe are due on April 15th. Your employer will give you a W-2 form. The W-2 tells how much money you earned last year and how much money the government withheld for taxes. If your taxes are simple, you can use a 1040EZ. You use this form to calculate the money that you need to pay or get back. When you get money back, it is called a *refund*.

☞ Compare Cultures

Make a diagram like the one below to compare how countries use taxes. Use the words in the vocabulary box to help you. Compare your diagram with a partner's.

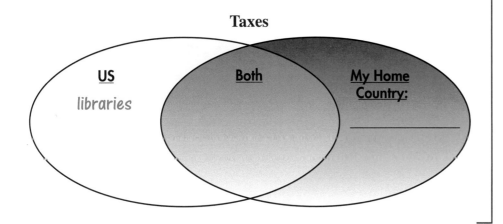

Taxes

Vocabulary

Listen and repeat. Circle new words. Get meanings from a classmate, your teacher, or a dictionary. Write the words and their meanings.

calculate

collect

owe

refund

federal

state

courthouse

fire fighter

military

police

welfare

_____
your word

One Step Up

List more things taxes pay for in the US. Which partner can list more things in three minutes?

Activity A   Work with your group. Find out about your community. Do you have to pay sales taxes? Make a list of things you pay taxes on. Make a list of things you don't have to pay taxes on. Talk to the class about your lists.

Activity B   Look at the tax table. How much federal tax do you have to pay if you earn . . .

$41,210 a year and you are single? _____

$41,425 a year and you are the head of your household? _____

$41,150 a year and you are married filing jointly? _____

$41,530 a year and you are married filing separately? _____

Tax Table					
If line 39 (taxable income) is—		And you are—			
At least	But less than	Single	Married filing jointly	Married filing separately	Head of a household
41,000		Your tax is —			
41,000	41,050	7,901	6,154	8,457	6,751
41,050	41,100	7,914	6,161	8,471	6,764
41,100	41,150	7,928	6,169	8,484	6,778
41,150	41,200	7,942	6,176	8,498	6,792
41,200	41,250	7,956	6,184	8,512	6,806
41,250	41,300	7,969	6,191	8,526	6,819
41,300	41,350	7,983	6,199	8,539	6,833
41,350	41,400	7,997	6,206	8,553	6,847
41,400	41,450	8,011	6,214	8,567	6,861
41,450	41,500	8,024	6,221	8,581	6,874
41,500	41,550	8,038	6,229	8,594	6,888

filing jointly = filling out the form together
head of household = a single person who works to support the family

TASK 3   Make a List of Tax Forms

Get a large envelope. Label it with the word "taxes" and write the year on the outside. With a small group, list all the tax forms and receipts you want to collect in the envelope. Copy the list onto the envelope. Think of a safe place to keep your envelope.

Calculate Taxes

Practice completing a 1040EZ Form for Puri Patel. Calculate how much federal income tax Puri has to pay or how much of a refund he will get.

Get Ready

Work in small groups. Get a copy of Form 1040EZ from your teacher. Look back at Puri's employment information. Puri Patel is a 33-year-old married man. His W-2 form stated that he earned $41,513 in wages. The income tax withheld was $8,162. His wife earned no income this year.

Do the Work

Complete the 1040EZ Form for Puri. Use the Tax Table on page 92 to calculate how much federal income tax he has to pay. Puri and Nadya want to file jointly. Will he receive a refund? Will he have to pay more taxes? What can he do next year?

Present Your Project

Compare your answers with another group. Are they the same?

Writing Extension Write a short letter to Puri from the IRS. Will he get good news or bad news? Share your letter with the class.

✂〰🖥 Technology Extra

Go to the IRS web site. Look for the latest tax forms and information. Practice completing the forms about your income.

Understanding Yourself

Learning Your Strengths

Work/School
1

Home
2

Community
3

◆ **Vocabulary** Words to describe people • Words to describe relationships

◆ **Language** Reflexive pronouns • Future with *will* (review) and *going to*

◆ **Pronunciation** Sounds of *u* • Sounds of *b* and *v*

◆ **Culture** Marriage in the US

How well do you know yourself?

Are Carlos and Donna going to have a good future together?

Think and Talk

1. Where are Carlos and his girlfriend?
2. What are they talking about?
3. Why is he excited?
4. How does Donna feel?
5. How would you feel in a similar situation?

Picture Dictionary   Listen and repeat. Circle new words.
Get meanings from a classmate, your teacher, or a dictionary.
Write the words and their meanings.

Adjectives That Describe People

artistic   intelligent

athletic   kind

Opposites

generous	selfish
honest	dishonest
outgoing	quiet
positive	negative

Gather Your Thoughts   Think about yourself. List the vocabulary
words you would use to describe yourself. Start with the word that best
describes you. End with the word that least describes you.

best
describe
least

What's the Problem?   What do you do well? What jobs are you
good at? What jobs are you bad at? Think or talk with a partner.

Setting Goals   Think about your answers to the questions above.
What can you do to understand yourself better? Check ✔ your goals.

- ❑ **1.** Learn more about myself.
- ❑ **2.** Learn about skills that are important in my life.
- ❑ **3.** Make a list of my strengths and weaknesses.
- ❑ **4.** Read and learn about relationships.
- ❑ **5.** Another goal: _____

Strengths and Weaknesses

◆ Find out about your strengths and weaknesses

◆ Use reflexive pronouns

| career |
| negotiate |

What do you do best? What do you need to improve?

◆ Reading Tip   One way to understand what you read is to think about how it relates to your own life. Think about *your* skills. Now study Carlos's skills inventory. Put a star next to two skills you do best. Circle two skills you need to improve.

Career Skills Inventory

This test will evaluate your skills and weaknesses in the workplace. Check whether each statement is true always, sometimes, or never.

	Always True	Sometimes	Never True
Communication			
I am a good listener.	☐	☑	☐
I am a good speaker.	☐	☑	☐
I can write my ideas well.	☐	☑	☐
Working with Others			
I enjoy working with other people.	☐	☑	☐
I am a good leader.	☑	☐	☐
I like to help others.	☑	☐	☐
Decision Making & Problem Solving			
I can use math to solve problems.	☐	☐	☑
I make decisions easily.	☐	☑	☐
I can negotiate to resolve conflicts.	☐	☐	☑
Learning			
I read to learn new things.	☐		
I enjoy doing research on the computer.	☑		
I like taking classes.	☐		

The inventory shows that I work well with other people.

Talk or Write

1. With a partner, talk about the meaning of each skill in the inventory. In your notebook, explain each skill in your own words.
2. Which skills do you need most in your job or family life?

Class Chat Walk around. Ask questions. Write answers.

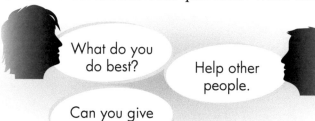

What do you do best?

Help other people.

Can you give an example?

What's your name?	What do you do best?	Can you give an example?
Carlos Cepeda	Help other people.	I coach a soccer team.

Grammar Talk: Reflexive Pronouns

I understand **myself** better after taking the inventory.

Do you know **yourself?**

Carlos is proud of **himself** because of his promotion.

What word part do you see in all the reflexive pronouns? Use reflexive pronouns when the same person or thing does the action and receives the action.

Vocabulary

Listen and repeat. Circle new words. Get meanings from a classmate, your teacher, or a dictionary. Write the words and their meanings.

communication

decision

example

leader

math

research

communicate

evaluate

improve

negotiate

solve

best

strongest

weakest

Pronunciation Target • Sounds of *u*

 Listen to your teacher or the audio.

Short *u*	Long *u*
public	humor
cup	huge
luck	use

With a partner practice saying the words. Then think of other words with u. Practice saying them and write them in a two-column chart in your notebook.

Activity A   Tell a partner about yourself. Tell one strength and one weakness.

What do you know about yourself?

I am good at solving problems, but I am not very good at working with people.

Activity B   **Class Chat Follow-Up** Write sentences in your notebook about your classmates.

Carlos knows himself better now. He is good at helping

other people.

Activity C   In your notebook, write sentences about people you know. What did they accomplish by themselves using their strengths?

Andrea took care of the problem at work by herself. She spoke

to her boss.

Now write sentences about yourself in your notebook. What can you do by yourself?

| by yourself |

 TASK 1 Evaluate Jobs for Your Skills

Look at the skills inventory on page 96. Write your strongest skill: communication, decision making, etc. Find other people in your class with the same strength. Discuss jobs that are good for you. Evaluate each job. Complete a chart like the one below.

Jobs	Positive	Negative
1. Manager	more money	more stress
2.		
3.		

Select one job. Make a presentation to the class. Tell why the job is good for you. Tell why it could be bad for you.

Coming Together

◆ Discuss relationships
◆ Learn about marriage and divorce in the US

| feeling |
| self-confidence |
| worry/worried |

Why do couples get angry?

◆ Listening Tip 🎧 Listening for feelings can help you understand what you hear. Now listen to the conversation between Carlos and Donna. Try to imagine what they are feeling. You can read the words on page 119.

Carlos and Donna need to be more sensitive with each other.

Talk or Write
1. What was Carlos worried about? Why?
2. What does Donna think?
3. Why are they angry?
4. How can they communicate better?

In the US   Marriage Is Not Easy!

Couples fall in love and get married, but many marriages end in divorce. The divorce rate in the US is very high. Relationships are not easy! Sometimes people are busy or stressed. Stress can cause conflict. To live and work together happily, people need to understand themselves. Then they can try to understand each other, their co-workers, their neighbors, and their spouses.

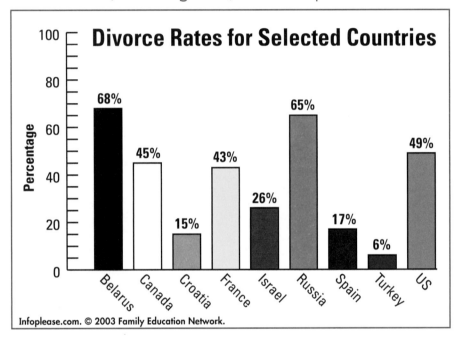

Divorce Rates for Selected Countries

Belarus 68%
Canada 45%
Croatia 15%
France 43%
Israel 26%
Russia 65%
Spain 17%
Turkey 6%
US 49%

Percentage

Infoplease.com. © 2003 Family Education Network.

☛ **Compare Cultures**

Is the divorce rate high or low in your home country? Why do you think people do or do not divorce in your country? In a group, talk about how marriage is the same or different in different countries.

Activity A   Work in a group of three. Students A and B talk. Student C listens to them. Student A talks about an imaginary or a real problem. Imagine a problem with your spouse, a co-worker, your boss, a neighbor, a friend, or a family member. Student B gives advice. Student C listens and then gives advice. Then exchange roles. Repeat until each group member has played all three roles.

100   *Unit 8 Lesson 2*

© NEW Readers Press. All rights reserved.

Vocabulary

Listen and repeat. Circle new words. Get meanings from a classmate, your teacher, or a dictionary. Write the words and their meanings.

describe

energetic
ideal
independent
sensitive

conflict
couple
divorce
feeling
marriage
relationship

_____
your word

Remember?
stress
stressed

Activity B   What are some ways you can improve your relationships?
Work with a partner. Check ✔ all that apply. Give examples.

❑ Talk about your feelings.
❑ Listen carefully.
❑ Join discussion groups.
❑ Go to counseling.
❑ Spend more time with others.

❑ Talk about problems with parents or friends.
❑ Talk with a spiritual leader.
❑ Watch self-help videos or read self-help books.
❑ Reduce the stress in your life.
❑ Other: _____

Activity C   Work in a small group. Read about Carlos and Donna.

Carlos Cepeda is ambitious, hard-working, and intelligent. He is also kind and generous. At times, he can be selfish.

Donna Sullivan is energetic and independent. She is athletic and outgoing.

With your group, create an imaginary, ideal person. What characteristics would your ideal person have? Make a list.

Our ideal person is _____ , _____ , _____

_____ , _____ , _____ .

TASK 2   Describe Good Relationships

In small groups, look at the chart below. Check *Yes* for things that are important in a relationship. Check *No* for things that are not good for a relationship. Talk about why. Complete the chart. Share with your class.

	accept
	criticize
	respect

Yes	No		Yes	No	
____	____	Good listening	____	____	Understanding yourself
____	____	Showing anger	____	____	Accepting differences
____	____	Hiding feelings	____	____	Never apologizing
____	____	Communicating openly	____	____	Criticizing
____	____	Showing feelings	____	____	Cooperating
____	____	Respecting other's opinions	____	____	Other: _____

Neighbors Helping Neighbors

◆ Talk about helping neighbors
◆ Use future tense with *will* (review) and *going to*

What important issues do you have in your neighborhood?

> association
> discuss
> maintenance

◆ Reading Tip   Focusing on specific details can help you understand what you read. As you read the following e-mail message, think about *what, when,* and *why.*

Reply   Reply All   Forward

To: Carlos Cepeda
From: Montopolis Neighborhood Association
Subject: Meeting

Please plan to attend the next Montopolis Neighborhood Association Meeting. The meeting will be held at the Town Hall on Wednesday, September 10, at 8:00 p.m. We really need your help. We will discuss these important issues: crime watch, children's safety, lawn maintenance, trash pick-up, and noise control. We will serve refreshments. Bring a guest! Everyone is welcome. Please come!

Now you know why I like to come here.

Yes, you love to be around other people.

Talk or Write

1. What is the e-mail announcing?
2. When is the meeting? Where is it?
3. Why is it important to attend?
4. What issues will the association discuss?

Remember?
neighborhood
volunteer

Class Chat   Walk around. Ask questions. Write the answers.

How will you help in your neighborhood?

I am going to talk to the neighbors on my block.

What neighborhood do you live in?	What's the main issue there?	How will you help?
South Central	loud music after 10:00 p.m.	talk to the neighbors

Vocabulary

Listen and repeat. Circle new words. Get meanings from a classmate, your teacher, or a dictionary. Write the words and their meanings.

block

crime

issue

lawn

noise

safety

trash

join

Grammar Talk: Future with *Will* and *Going To*

How **will** you help your neighbor?	How **are** you **going to** help your neighbor?
I **will** join the association.	I **am going to** join the association.
We **will** take turns watching the block.	We **are going to** take turns watching the block.
Our children **will** be safe.	Our children **are going to** be safe.
Donna **will not** volunteer this time.	Donna **isn't going to** volunteer this time.

What are the two ways of talking about the future?

take turns

Pronunciation Target • Sounds of *b* and *v*

🎧 *Listen to your teacher or the audio. Listen for the difference between* b *and* v.

block	voice
neighbor	divorce
berry	volunteer

Find other words with b *and* v. *Write them in your notebook. Practice pronouncing them with a partner.*

Activity A Write sentences about the things that you will do to have a better relationship with your neighbors. Use *will*. Then write sentences with *going to*.

1. <u>We will try to know our neighbors better.</u>

   <u>We are going to try to know our neighbors better.</u>

2. _____

   _____

3. _____

   _____

Now work with a partner. Complete a diagram like this one.

One Step Up
Write about what you are going to do to make your relationships with your neighbors better.

Things we will do

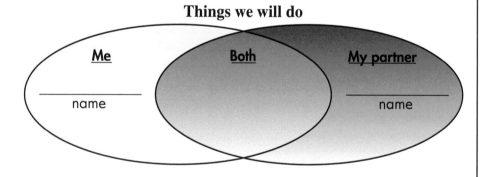

Me

Both

My partner

_____ name

_____ name

 TASK 3 Solve a Problem

Choose a problem below. Work in a small group. Talk about what you can do and what you should not do. Write a plan to solve the problem.

mow lawns

Problem 1	Problem 2	Problem 3
You will have a big party on Sunday. There will be cars, music, and a lot of noise. What will you do to prevent conflict with your neighbors?	There is a lot of crime in your neighborhood. Some neighbors want to move away. You want to stay and make things better. What will you do?	Some of your neighbors have beautiful lawns. Some do not. One neighbor wants everyone to clean up trash and mow lawns every week. What do you think of this issue? Is it important? What will you do?

Describe Yourself

Find your strengths and weaknesses on a skills inventory.

Get Ready

Look back at your work for Task 1. What did you decide was your strongest area? Why?

Do the Work

Get a copy of the skills inventory from your teacher. Find the skills you are strongest in. Make a list of jobs or tasks that would make good use of your skills. Find the skills you are weakest in. Make a list of things you can do to improve these skills. How will you improve your weakest skills? Use a chart like this one. Write a plan in your notebook.

My Strongest Skills	Jobs I Can Do Well
1. leadership	1. team leader or supervisor
2. helpful/friendly	2. customer service
3. computer research	3. information technology
My Weakest Skills	**What I Can Do to Improve**
1. listening	1. Be more patient and attentive.
2. math	2. Take a math class.
3. negotiating	3. Read about negotiation skills.

Present Your Project

Show your skills inventory to your group. Talk about your strengths. Give an example of two or three of your strongest skills.

✎💻 Technology Extra

Look for a search engine. Type in "skills inventory." Find a web site that offers a free skills inventory. Complete the inventory and share it with the class.

It Takes a Team

Celebrating Success

Work/School
1

Home
2

Community
3

◆ **Vocabulary** Celebrations • Skills for working with other people

◆ **Language** Direct and indirect object pronouns • Simple past tense of regular and irregular verbs (review)

◆ **Pronunciation** Sound of the *-tion* ending • Sounds of *r*

◆ **Culture** Celebrations in the US

> celebrate
> surprise
> worth it

> Surprise! Happy 80th Birthday!

> It was difficult to get our family to work together.

> But we did it, Mai Lin, and our teamwork was worth it!

What do you celebrate?

A family plans together to celebrate a good long life.

Think and Talk

1. Where is Mai Lin? What's happening?
2. How does her father look? Why?
3. What was the problem?
4. Did you ever work on a team to plan a celebration?

Gather Your Thoughts

What do you celebrate? Who helps plan your celebrations? What does everyone need to do? Make an idea map. Here is an example.

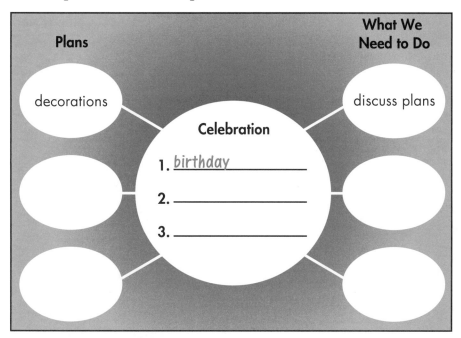

Plans

decorations

Celebration

1. birthday
2. _____
3. _____

What We Need to Do

discuss plans

Vocabulary

Listen and repeat. Circle new words. Get meanings from a classmate, your teacher, or a dictionary. Write the words and their meanings.

agree/disagree

celebrate/celebration

decorate/decoration

discuss/discussion

speak/speech

event

suggestion

team/teamwork

_____
your word

What's the Problem?

Do you ever disagree with other people? How can you work together to plan an event? Think or talk with a partner.

Setting Goals

Think about your answers to the questions above. What can you do when you disagree with other people? Check ✔ your goals

❑ **1.** Discuss ideas.
❑ **2.** Listen carefully to everyone's suggestions.
❑ **3.** Make suggestions.
❑ **4.** Cooperate with the group.
❑ **5.** Take responsibility.
❑ **6.** Another goal: _____

cooperate = work with

Working Together

◆ Talk about strategies for success

◆ Use direct and indirect object pronouns

| confidence |
| factory |
| production |

What are your main strategies for success?

◆ Listening Tip 🎧 When you listen, think about your own life. This will help you understand what you hear. Now listen to the conversation between Mai Lin and her boss. What would you say if your boss asked you to speak to other employees? You can read the words on page 119.

Mai Lin's boss congratulates her for her good work.

Talk or Write

1. What is the boss talking about?
2. What is Mai Lin's position in the factory store?
3. Why should she be proud of herself?
4. What does her boss ask her to do?
5. Did something like this ever happen to you?

Class Chat   Walk around. Ask questions. Write answers.

When did you work on a team?

We planned a class visit to the library.

What's your name?	When did you work on a team?	What was good or bad?
Renee	We planned a class visit to the library.	Our team agreed on the day but not on the time.

Vocabulary

Listen and repeat. Circle new words. Get meanings from a classmate, your teacher, or a dictionary. Write the words and their meanings.

congratulate/ congratulations

gift

strategy

success

proud

successful

Grammar Talk: Direct and Indirect Object Pronouns

1. Who planned the party for your father? My family planned **it** for **him.**
2. We all bought **him** a gift, and my aunt gave **it** to **him.**
3. Mai Lin values the team members' suggestions. She thanked **us** for **them.**
4. Her boss asked **her** to make a presentation. She agreed to do **it** for **him.**

Pronouns are small words used in place of nouns.
In example 1, it = the party.

Activity A   To whom or to what does each pronoun in the Grammar Talk refer?

1. it = _____the party_____   him = _____

2. him = _____   it = _____   him = _____

3. us = _____   them = _____

4. her = _____   it = _____   him = _____

Pronunciation Target • Sound of *-tion* ending

🎧 *Listen to your teacher or the audio.*

celebration   decoration   suggestion

Repeat the words. Find more words that end in -tion. *Write them in your notebook. Practice saying the words with a partner.*

Activity B   Class Chat Follow-Up   Write sentences about your classmates.

1. Renee helped plan a visit to the library. Everyone wanted to

    go on Friday, but they did not agree on the time.

2. _____

    _____

3. _____

    _____

Activity C   Work with a partner. Talk about a successful event that you helped plan. Tell why you did it. In your notebook, write about your event and your partner's event.

I planned a celebration for my teacher. I did it for her.

Write the pronouns and to what or whom they refer.

it = a celebration, her = my teacher

TASK 1   Describe Successful Team Planning

Work with a small group. Think of two examples of successful teamwork in your life. Tell about one example in your personal life and one in your school or work life. Write details in a chart like this one.

	Personal Event	School or Work Event
What		
Who		
When		
Where		
Why		

Sharing Success

◆ Talk about teamwork

◆ Use simple past tense of regular and irregular verbs (review)

What kinds of things do you like to share with family or friends?

◆ Reading Tip   People learn from experience. What are some things you learned that make you successful? Now read Mai Lin's speech. It tells what *she* learned from experience.

I have good news! My boss praised me on my teamwork.

I finished my speech. What do you think?

Sharing success makes it better.

When my family and I came to this country, we were very scared. We were also sad because we left behind people we loved. We found new friends in the US. We learned that we were not alone.

I understood at that time how important it was to work as a team. We always showed respect to members of our family, especially the older people. If we listen to them, we can learn from them.

As a team leader at work, I did the things that I learned from my family. I listened to other people, and I respected their opinions. I tried to be honest. I expected them to act the same way with me. We all were proud of our work, and we wanted to earn the respect of others. Those are the secrets of our success!

Talk or Write

1. What did Mai Lin learn from her family?
2. What are her ideas for successful teamwork?
3. What did you learn in your home country that helped you in the US?

Class Chat   Walk around. Ask questions. Write the answers.

What did you do at home to get along?

I listened to my daughter's opinion.

Name	What did you do at home to get along?	What happened?
Shana	listened to my daughter's opinion	We didn't argue.

Grammar Talk: Simple Past Tense of Regular and Irregular Verbs

Mai Lin **learned** from her experiences.

Many people **helped** her family to survive in the US.

They **found** some wonderful new friends.

Her team members **were** proud of their work.

How do you form the past tense of most verbs? Can you think of other irregular verbs?

Vocabulary

Listen and repeat. Circle new words. Get meanings from a classmate, your teacher, or a dictionary. Write the words and their meanings.

argue

expect

praise

respect

trust

opinion

solution

_____
your word

Pronunciation Target • Sounds of *r*

🎧 *Listen to your teacher or the audio.*

respect   right   argue   proud   praise   trust

Practice saying the sounds of r. Practice the words with a partner. Think of other words with r. Write them in your notebook and practice saying them.

Activity A   Class Chat Follow-Up   Write sentences about your classmates in your notebook. Follow the model.

Shana listened to her daughter's opinion. Then they didn't argue.

Activity B   Here are Mai Lin's notes on being a good team leader.

	A good team leader...
○	• listens with understanding • is open to new ideas • discusses problems • trusts the group • communicates honestly • makes good decisions • expects cooperation • finds solutions

Work with a partner. Think of a time you had a family, work, or community team project. Write some things people did to cooperate. Then write some things they did not do.

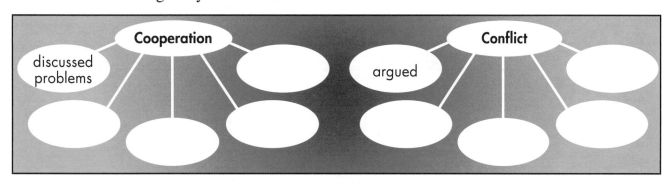

Activity C   Work in your group. How much do you think it cost to have Mai Lin's father's surprise party? Estimate the cost and sales tax for a party in your area.

Number of people: _____   Decorations: _____

Food: _____   Location: _____

Drinks: _____

 TASK 2   Write a Group Speech about Teamwork

Work in a small group. Write a speech about teamwork. One person visits a different group and reads the speech. The new group makes positive comments and gives some suggestions for improvement. Return to your group. Revise your group's speech.

> revise

Positive Comments	Suggestions for Improvement
meaningful	more details
emotional	speak louder
well organized	speak slower
interesting	practice pronunciation

One Step Up
One person from each group reads the revised speech to the class.

Enjoying Success

◆ Discuss ways to celebrate

◆ Learn about holidays in the US

| coupon |
| gift certificate |
| reward |

How do you celebrate an important event?

◆ Reading Tip Before you read a ticket, a certificate, or a coupon, scan it to find the most important information for you. Now read the ticket, certificate, and coupon below. Find the most important information in each one.

9

Ticket No. 209632

To: _____
From: _____

209632

$15 FUN CITY $15
AMUSEMENT PARK
Includes 5 rides • Valid to: Dec. 12, 2009.
Please show at the gate. No refunds.

MONEY SAVING COUPON for
BETTER BARGAINS SUPERSTORE
SAVE 30%
on
VA

Gift Certificate to Richie's
THE RIGHT RESTAURANT
FOR YOU!
Up to $25 off dinner for two.
Not valid on weekends

Mai Lin's company rewarded her team members for their hard work.

Talk or Write
1. How many rides can Mai Lin go on with this ticket?
2. What is the value of the gift certificate?
3. How much money can Mai Lin save with the coupon?

In the US   *What Do We Celebrate?*

The 4th of July, or Independence Day, celebrates the signing of the Declaration of Independence in 1776. It celebrates the *birth* of the United States. Many people join friends, family, and neighbors in a picnic because the holiday is in the summer. Everyone enjoys fireworks at night!

Thanksgiving is another US holiday. It is a day to share a big meal and give thanks. Many people eat roast turkey. This holiday celebrates the first settlers to North America. Native Americans helped them. In the fall, the settlers had a feast and invited the Native Americans to join them.

On Halloween, children in the US dress in costumes. They go to neighbors' homes and ask for candy. People decorate with pumpkins and witches.

Americans also celebrate birthdays. Children often have big birthday parties. There is a cake with candles. Guests bring gifts. Everyone sings "Happy Birthday to You."

☛ Compare Cultures

What is one traditional celebration in your country?
- Take notes. When did you celebrate? Where? What did you do? Was there special food? Music? Decorations?
- Then talk with a partner.
- Tell your partner how you celebrated the last time.

Vocabulary

Listen and repeat. Circle new words. Get meanings from a classmate, your teacher, or a dictionary. Write the words and their meanings.

- birth
- birthday
- feast
- guest
- holiday
- invite
- invitation
- occasion

_____
your word

candy
costume
fireworks
Native American
pumpkin
roast
settler
turkey
witch

One Step Up
Tell the class about your country's celebration.

Activity A   Work with a partner. List your favorite celebrations.
What did you do last year to celebrate these events? Complete the chart.

Celebration	What I Did Last Year
4th of July	went to the park with my family

Activity B   Work in a group of four. Talk about your activities this
past weekend. Talk about the things you liked and did not like about
the weekend. Complete a chart like this one.

One Step Up
Tell the class about your last weekend.

Activity	Liked	Did Not Like
1. I went to a movie.	I was with my boyfriend.	The movie was too long.
2.		
3.		
4.		

TASK 3   Write a Speech about Success

Go back to your success stories in Task 1. Choose one. Write a speech
describing your success. Include the reasons you were successful.
Show your speech to a partner. Make suggestions to improve your
partner's speech.

Present a Success Story

Present a success story to the class.

Get Ready

Think of a success story in your life. It could be the one that you selected for Task 3 or a different one. Collect things related to your success:

- photos
- objects
- tickets, flyers
- cards, invitations
- other: _____

Do the Work

1. Revise the speech you wrote for Task 3 or write a new speech. Use the cards from your teacher. Tell about what you and others did to cause the success. Tell how you celebrated.
2. Make a poster. Use pictures. Use other things that help make your speech interesting.

When and Where You Celebrated

We all went to Fun City last weekend. We had a great time!

I took my parents to Richie's for dinner on Thursday night. I wanted to share my success with them.

Present Your Project

Give your speech to the class.

Writing Extension   Write sentences about each of the speeches presented. Write the name of the speaker. Say something positive. Then say something to help improve the speech.

Technology Extra

Create a presentation on the computer, or write the speech on your word processor. Try to include color, pictures, and different types of letters.

Listening Scripts

UNIT 1
Time for a Change

Lesson 3, page 18

Interviewer: Good morning, Mr. Gorovoy.

Nicholas: Good morning, sir.

Interviewer: I see from your application that you work in the auto industry.

Nicholas: Yes, sir, but I'm interested in becoming an electrician.

Interviewer: You're in the right place. Our company is growing. We need ambitious workers who want to learn. Why do you think you can be a good electrician?

Nicholas: Well, I helped my wife's uncle wire his house. I learn quickly, and I can read technical directions.

Interviewer: There are many places to work. Why are you interested in our company?

Nicholas: I know that you have a job-training program.

Interviewer: Yes, we have an 18-month electrician's-helper program.

Nicholas: I want to work and go to school at the same time.

Interviewer: Our program pays you during your training. And we have an opening. Are you interested?

Nicholas: Yes, I am! How much does it pay?

Interviewer: This job pays $700 a week. We also have excellent benefits. When can you start?

Nicholas: I can start in two weeks.

Interviewer: Good. Welcome to the team!

Nicholas: Thank you very much.

UNIT 2
New Beginnings

Lesson 1, page 24

Hi Mom and Grandma, this is Raisa. Sorry we missed you. Luisa and I stayed at school for swimming practice. Our coach ordered pizza. We want to stay and eat with the team. Call the school if we need to come home for dinner, 555-3333. Love ya. Bye.

Activity C, page 26

Ritza: Mom, are you sorry that you came to the United States?

Fotini: Oh, no. But sometimes I'm not sure that I can help.

Ritza: You help us so much! The girls and I are very happy that you are here.

UNIT 3
Balancing Your Life

Lesson 2, page 39

Silvia: I don't feel well. I have a headache and a stomachache. I also have a sore throat. I'm tired, but I don't sleep well.

Doctor: Hmmm. Let's see what's going on. Your throat looks bad. You probably have an infection. The nurse will do a test to be sure. I'm going to get you an antibiotic. Take this prescription to the pharmacy. Be sure to follow the instructions—one pill every six hours, OK? Now, tell me about your life.

Silvia: Well, . . . I work six days a week in a laundry room. I study at night to learn English. I also take care of my family. I cook, clean, drive my children to school, and help them with homework.

Doctor: That's a lot! Can your husband do some of the work at home? Talk to him. Be sure that he really understands. Your children probably could help you too.

Silvia: It's difficult for me to say that I can't do everything.

Doctor: I know. Also, try to exercise at least four times a week. Walking is good. You need to relax, Silvia. You need to balance your life.

UNIT 4
Making a Plan for Your Money

Lesson 2, page 51

Bank Clerk: Good morning. My name is Cathy Reynolds. How can I help you?

Joseph: Good morning. My name is Joseph Delva. I need to open an account.

Bank Clerk: A checking account or savings account?

Joseph: Both. What do I have to do?

Bank Clerk: You have to fill out an application form. And you must provide a photo ID. Now, how much will you deposit in each account? You must deposit a minimum of $25.00 to open the savings account.

Joseph: Here is my paycheck. I'll deposit 10% into my savings and the rest in the checking account.

Bank Clerk: I see that you already endorsed your check. Never endorse the check before you come to the bank. Anyone can cash an endorsed check! If you must endorse the check, write *for deposit only* under your signature.

Joseph: OK. That's good to know. When does my statement come?

Bank Clerk: You will get a bank statement the first week of every month. Use it to balance your checkbook.

Joseph: How do I balance my checkbook?

Bank Clerk: This flyer explains

how to balance your checkbook. If you have any problems, just come back. I'll help you.

UNIT 5
Bargain Shopping

Lesson 2, page 63
Better Bargains Superstore Back-to-School Sale!
Don't miss the Back-to-School Sale at Better Bargains Superstore today and tomorrow. Everything is on sale! Nothing is full price. Stop by and save on our products.
Brand name clothes —
Sneakers and sandals —
School supplies —
And much, much more!
You will also find great bargains in our appliance and furniture departments. It's always easier and cheaper to shop with us at Better Bargains Superstore, 2555 East Gulf Freeway. Come on in today for the super sale of the year!

UNIT 6
Equal Rights

Lesson 1, page 72
Ben Sanders: Good morning. Are you Amara Mirembe? Sit down please.
Amara: Good morning, sir. Thank you.
Ben Sanders: I see here you're applying for the machine repair position.
Amara: Yes, sir. I repaired machines in a textile plant in my country. May I show you my recommendation?
Ben Sanders: That's OK. Here you should try to start out as an operator.
Amara: But, sir, I think I could do a very good job for you as a machine repairperson.

Ben Sanders: Sure, sure. We'll call you if we have the right job. Thank you for coming in.

UNIT 7
Paying Taxes

Activity B, page 89
Form W-4 tells how much money to withhold from your paycheck for taxes. You write how many allowances you want to claim. If no one else can claim you as a dependent, you enter 1 for yourself. If you are married, you may want to claim your spouse too. You can claim any children you support as dependents. When you claim more dependents, you take home more net pay. However, you may have to pay more taxes to the IRS in April.

Lesson 3, page 90
Nadya: Would you like some hot mint tea?
Puri: Yes, thank you. I am beginning to understand the tax system in the United States.
Nadya: You can do it. You are an accountant!
Puri: That helps, but everything is different here. I have my W-2 form from work. I need to complete our 1040.
Nadya: Do we owe money?
Puri: I don't think so. I think we will get a refund.
Nadya: I hope so! We need extra money.

UNIT 8
Understanding Yourself

Lesson 2, page 99
Carlos: I took a skills inventory today.
Donna: How did you do?
Carlos: It showed that my strength is working with other people. I'm worried that I won't

be the best person for the new position.
Donna: Carlos, you need to have more self-confidence.
Carlos: The position is in the research department. I am going to work alone.
Donna: Carlos, don't be so negative! You worry too much.
Carlos: Donna, you aren't listening to me. I am under a lot of stress planning our future together.
Donna: You're not the only one! I had a hard day at work myself!

UNIT 9
It Takes a Team

Lesson 1, page 108
Mr. Cohen: Congratulations, Mai Lin. Your team had the highest sales total this month for our factory store.
Mai Lin: Thank you, sir. I am really proud of them.
Mr. Cohen: You should be. But you should also be proud of yourself.
Mai Lin: All four of us worked together.
Mr. Cohen: Maybe you can speak at our next employees' meeting. You could tell them about your strategies for success.
Mai Lin: I am worried they won't understand me. My English pronunciation is not very good.
Mr. Cohen: Have more confidence in yourself! You're a great team leader, and you can share your ideas with other employees.
Mai Lin: I will try to do it for you, Mr. Cohen.

The US

Washington
(WA)

Montana
(MT)

North Dakota
(ND)

Minne...
(MN

Oregon
(OR)

Idaho
(ID)

South Dakota
(SD)

Wyoming
(WY)

Nebraska
(NE)

Nevada
(NV)

Utah
(UT)

Colorado
(CO)

Kansas
(KS)

California
(CA)

• Los Angeles

Arizona
(AZ)

New Mexico
(NM)

Oklahoma
(OK)

*Pacific
Ocean*

Texas
(TX)

MEXICO

Houston •

Alaska
(AK)

Hawaii
(HI)

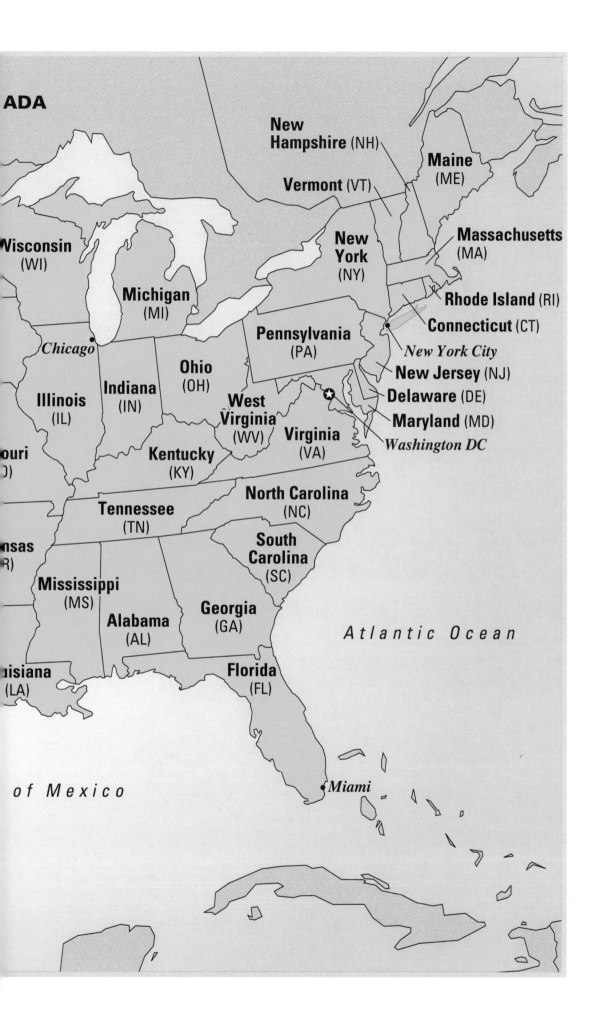

ADA

New Hampshire (NH)

Vermont (VT)

Maine (ME)

New York (NY)

Massachusetts (MA)

Rhode Island (RI)

Connecticut (CT)

New York City

New Jersey (NJ)

Delaware (DE)

Maryland (MD)

Washington DC

Wisconsin (WI)

Michigan (MI)

Chicago

Pennsylvania (PA)

Ohio (OH)

Illinois (IL)

Indiana (IN)

West Virginia (WV)

Virginia (VA)

ouri)

Kentucky (KY)

North Carolina (NC)

Tennessee (TN)

nsas R)

South Carolina (SC)

Mississippi (MS)

Alabama (AL)

Georgia (GA)

Atlantic Ocean

isiana (LA)

Florida (FL)

of Mexico

Miami

The World

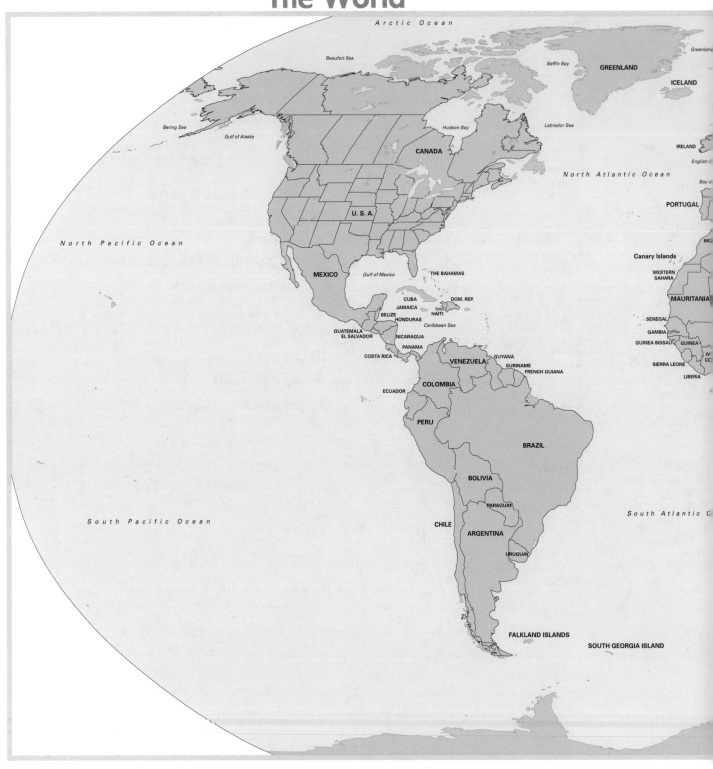

Arctic Ocean

Beaufort Sea

Baffin Bay

GREENLAND

Greenland

ICELAND

Bering Sea

Gulf of Alaska

Hudson Bay

Labrador Sea

CANADA

IRELAND

English

North Atlantic Ocean

Bay of

North Pacific Ocean

U.S.A.

PORTUGAL

MO

Canary Islands

MEXICO

Gulf of Mexico

THE BAHAMAS

**WESTERN
SAHARA**

MAURITANIA

CUBA

DOM. REP.

SENEGAL

JAMAICA

BELIZE

HAITI

GAMBIA

HONDURAS

Caribbean Sea

GUINEA BISSAU

GUINEA

GUATEMALA

NICARAGUA

EL SALVADOR

IV
CC

SIERRA LEONE

COSTA RICA

PANAMA

VENEZUELA

GUYANA

LIBERIA

SURINAME

COLOMBIA

FRENCH GUIANA

ECUADOR

PERU

BRAZIL

BOLIVIA

PARAGUAY

South Pacific Ocean

South Atlantic O

CHILE

ARGENTINA

URUGUAY

FALKLAND ISLANDS

SOUTH GEORGIA ISLAND

Months and Days

Months	Abbreviations		Days	Abbreviations
1. January	Jan.		Sunday	Sun.
2. February	Feb.		Monday	Mon.
3. March	Mar.		Tuesday	Tues.
4. April	Apr.		Wednesday	Wed.
5. May	May		Thursday	Thurs.
6. June	Jun.		Friday	Fri.
7. July	Jul.		Saturday	Sat.
8. August	Aug.			
9. September	Sept.			
10. October	Oct.			
11. November	Nov.			
12. December	Dec.			

August 2004

Sun.	Mon.	Tues.	Wed.	Thurs.	Fri.	Sat.
1	2	3	4	5	6	7
8	9	10	11	12	13	14
15	16	17	18	19	20	21
22	23	24	25	26	27	28
29	30	31				

US Holidays

Day	Date
New Year's Day	January 1
Martin Luther King Day	January 15*
Presidents' Day	third Monday in February
Memorial Day	May 30*
Independence Day	July 4
Labor Day	first Monday in September
Veterans Day	November 11
Thanksgiving	fourth Thursday in November
Christmas	December 25

* Observed on the closest Monday.

Irregular Past Tense Verbs

am/is/are	was/were	leave	left
bring	brought	make	made
build	built	put	put
buy	bought	read	read
can	could	see	saw
choose	chose	sell	sold
come	came	send	sent
do	did	spend	spent
drive	drove	swim	swam
eat	ate	take	took
feel	felt	teach	taught
find	found	tell	told
get	got	think	thought
give	gave	understand	understood
go	went	wear	wore
have	had	win	won
hide	hid	withdraw	withdrew
know	knew	write	wrote

Metric Conversions

To Convert	To	Multiply by
LENGTH		
meters	feet	3.281
kilometers	miles	0.62
LIQUID		
liters	quarts	1.057
liters	gallons	.0264
WEIGHT		
grams	ounces	0.0353
kilograms	pounds	2.2046
TEMPERATURE		
Celsius	Fahrenheit	multiply by 1.8, then add 32

To Convert	To	Multiply by
LENGTH		
feet	meters	.03048
miles	kilometers	1.609
LIQUID		
quarts	liters	0.946
gallons	liters	3.785
WEIGHT		
ounces	grams	28.35
pounds	kilograms	0.4536
TEMPERATURE		
Fahrenheit	Celsius	subtract 32, then multiply by 0.555

Writing Checklists

Writing Checklist for Sentences

❏ **1.** <u>D</u>id I capitalize the first word of every sentence?

❏ **2.** Did I end every sentence with a period (.), question mark (?), or exclamation point (!)?

❏ **3.** Did I ~~used~~ use correct grammar?

❏ **4.** Did I check my ~~speling~~ spelling?

❏ **5.** Is my handwriting neat and easy to read?

Writing Checklist for Paragraphs

❏ **1.** Did I think about the topic before writing?

❏ **2.** Did I take notes about my ideas before I started writing?

❏ **3.** Did I write a clear sentence to express my main idea?

❏ **4.** Did I write sentences with details to explain the main idea?

❏ **5.** Did I use clear and interesting examples, reasons, and facts?

❏ **6.** Did all my sentences relate to the main idea?

❏ **7.** Did I write in a logical order?

❏ **8.** Did I check each of my sentences using the Checklist for Sentences?

Topics

Grammar and Pronunciation

A

adjectives
  comparative, 61
  descriptive, 95
  order of, 88

B

be, simple present tense, 16

C

can, *cannot*, and *can't*, 13
compound sentences
  with *and* or *but*, 37
  with *and . . . too* and with *or*, 67

D

do and *does* in yes/no questions and
  answers, 40

F

future with *will* and *going to*, 103

H

have, simple present tense, 16
have to, 49

I

intonation
  in compound sentences, 37
  in statements and questions, 16

M

modals: *may*, *should*, *could*, *would*, 73
must, 49

P

past continuous, 79
past tense (simple)
  of irregular verbs, 28, 112, 125
  of regular verbs, 25, 112
present continuous, 79
pronouns
  direct and indirect object, 109
  reflexive, 97

R

reductions, 79

S

sentence stress, 13
sounds
  of *a*, 73
  of *b* and *v*, 103
  of *ch* and *sh*, 49
  of *e*, 85
  of *i*, 40
  of *o*, 29
  of *r*, 112
  of *s* and *st*, 67
  of simple past-tense endings, 25
  of *t* and *d*, 88
  of *th*, 61
  of the *–tion* ending, 110
  of *u*, 97
syllable stress, 55

V

verbs followed by infinitives, 85

W

wh- questions and answers, 52
will, *have to*, and *must*, 49